D0852800

Relationship Recipes

GIVING UP
JUNK-FOOD
RELATIONSHIPS

Relationship Recipes

GIVING UP
JUNK-FOOD
RELATIONSHIPS

Recipes for Healthy Choices

Donna Barnes
Life & Relationship Coach

iUniverse, Inc.
Bloomington

Giving Up Junk-Food Relationships
Recipes for Healthy Choices

Copyright © 2013 Donna Barnes

iUniverse books may be ordered through booksellers or by contacting:

iUniverse
1663 Liberty Drive
Bloomington, IN 47403
www.iuniverse.com
1-800-Authors (1-800-288-4677)

Front cover image credit: McMillan Digital Art/Photodisc/Getty Images

ISBN: 978-1-4759-7278-8 (sc)
ISBN: 978-1-4759-7277-1 (hc)
ISBN: 978-1-4759-7276-4 (e)

Library of Congress Control Number: 2013901114

Printed in the United States of America

iUniverse rev. date: 1/25/2013

This book is dedicated to all my previous junk-food partners who helped me learn how to become a well-balanced meal.

Thank you to my brother John for helping me brainstorm the food metaphor concept. I love you.

Thank you to my cousin Bruce Logan for your awesome illustrations.

And thank you to all my family, friends and clients for your support.

Contents

CONTENTS

Preface:

The Food of Love

You are what you eat, right? You likely know from experience that when you select healthy, well-balanced meals, you look and feel great, just as when you opt to fill up on junk food, though you may enjoy it in the moment, you probably don't feel so great afterward. Your health depends on what you choose to consume and how active you are. What about relationships? How are you supposed to know what will make you feel good and what will make you feel lousy? Well, surprise: the same rules that work with food also apply to relationships. What you put in is what you get out. Your happiness in a relationship depends on the choices you make.

The purpose of this book is to help you make better relationship choices.

I'm guessing you've already picked up on my metaphor: I'm going to equate specific foods with different types of relationships to make it easier for you to determine what is good for you and what's definitely bad. Naturally, a healthy, lasting relationship is a well-balanced meal. The Relationship Pyramid (see page 200) will outline the ingredients a healthy meal should contain. Dysfunctional affairs that are exciting when they start but ultimately become bad for you are junk-food relationships. Junk-food comes in many different containers; I'm going to help you lose your appetite for all of it.

These pages are not intended as ammunition for blaming your partner (or men or women in general). Blame is a key ingredient of junk-food. I'm going to ask you to take a look at yourself and take responsibility for your own actions, because if you do find (or have) a well-balanced meal, you'll want to make sure you don't burn it or let it spoil.

This book is intended for both women and men, either gay or straight.

Since my metaphor uses different types of food to represent people, I have frequently used the word "meal" as a nondifferential noun to replace the word "man" or "woman".

Note: Throughout this book are personal stories about my clients, friends, and associates. All names and personally identifying information has been changed to protect the confidentiality of the individuals mentioned.

Introduction:

What Is Emotional Junk-Food?

We all have our favorite drive-thru or take-out meal. A burger and fries can taste really good when you're out and about or in the airport rushing to get on a flight. It might even be a guilty pleasure that you go out of your way to devour. Sometimes when your stomach is growling out loud, you'll simply settle for what's readily available to satisfy your hunger.

How do you typically feel shortly after indulging your craving? Do you feel a little bloated? A little nauseated? Maybe you have some heartburn. Do you feel guilty and wish you had eaten something healthy instead? And have you noticed what happens to that scrumptious fast food when it cools off and isn't hot anymore? It's pretty nasty, isn't it?

Well, bad relationships are pretty much the same as junk food. They usually start out with a hunger or craving for companionship, but if this healthy craving escalates into loneliness and neediness, such people tend to make bad choices. They might just grab whoever's available or seek out a particular type that at first glance always appears appetizing. When it's hot, it's fabulous! It's exciting and fun—very enjoyable. But as the euphoria of the new relationship starts to wear off and the "can't get enough of you" passion cools down, what's left isn't exactly satisfying. Sometimes it's even harmful, and the long-term effects can be devastating. (Ever see *Fast Food Nation*?[1])

---

[1] *Fast Food Nation* is a 2006 American/British drama directed by Richard Linklater that examines the local and global influence of the US fast-food industry.

The difference between consuming *actual* junk food and indulging in *emotional* junk-food is that with food, at least you usually know what you're consuming isn't really good for you. With relationships it's not always as easy to tell it's not good for you until you've already digested a lot of it. As a relationship coach, I see a lot of people who don't really know if their relationship is right for them. I even see people who are in downright toxic relationships but don't know it, or refuse to acknowledge it. Many people think they know, or at least have an idea of, what they want in a relationship. But most people don't know what they *don't* want in a relationship until they've experienced it and didn't like it. I think knowing what you don't want in a partner is more important. This book is intended to empower you with knowledge—to help you create virtual nutrition labels for potential partners and make healthier relationship choices.

My greatest hope is to prevent you from suffering through a long list of dysfunctional "been there done that" liaisons to acquire knowledge, as I did. I always thought I was a great catch, and I hope you think you are a great catch as well. But if you're reading this book, your relationships probably aren't working out the way you want them to. They weren't working for me either, until I realized I needed to change some behavior. I was junk-food, and I learned that the hard way.

At age eighteen, my modeling agency got me an apartment in New York City. I was thrilled to be in the heart of America's biggest singles scene. I felt like a kid in a candy store! Parties, late night clubs, even in the dressing rooms of my modeling and acting bookings, I saw and heard a lot of dating tales and disasters. Personally, I was a serial monogamist (always had a boyfriend); I didn't want to be alone. But I never managed to make the *right* choices. My friends and family were frequently concerned. When you're in love (or think you are), you don't want to listen to anything negative. You certainly can't *hear* it. I made it through my twenties thinking I was doing okay. Then I turned thirty and had my heart broken for the first time. I was blindsided, actually, and I was having a hard time catching my breath. I was left questioning, "Why doesn't he want me anymore?" For the first time, I started to think, *What's wrong with me?*

A lot was wrong with me. Not just to suit any guy; negative behavior was affecting my life. It just took a guy to make me see that. I then had an epiphany: If I was ever going to have a healthy relationship, I needed to learn exactly what one was. A girlfriend turned me on to self-help books, and I discovered knowledge was the only thing that made me feel better. I became a knowledge junkie. I enlisted the help of a great therapist and serendipitously began a new career.

After years of dating without becoming someone's exclusive girlfriend, pining over a man I couldn't have (at least not full-time), starring in a reality show,[2] cohosting a talk show,[3] and writing a magazine column,[4] New York City started to call me "the real-life Carrie Bradshaw."[5] I have to admit that the title fit. I finally learned how to *enjoy* being alone; and then I met a wonderful well-balanced meal. In 2006, I enrolled at New York University[6] to officially become a life coach. Clients frequently tell me I give them a unique perspective—a combination of practical hindsight, intelligence, and academic knowledge. It's incredibly validating when they call to simply say, "You were right!" I can't help but think, "It's about time I got it right." Almost three decades later, I feel I have *earned* the title of dating and relationship expert. My favorite part is helping people make better choices than I did.

As a teenage model whose only income came from what she looked like, I was obsessed with working out and trying to eat right. I'm from Philadelphia, and cheesesteaks and hoagies (which come on a twelve-inch Italian roll) were my favorite comfort food. It was a constant battle between enjoying what I ate or enjoying how I looked. At the same time, I was struggling with my relationships. I had no idea what boundaries were, and looking back, I definitely had a few "What was I thinking?" relationships. If I had thought then to put a food value on men, I would have known exactly whom to indulge in and whom to throw away. That's how the idea for this book was born. Like attracts like; therefore, you are who you meet, just as you are what you eat. I'm going to give you a detailed nutrition label for all the most common—and some obscure—

---

[2] *Single in the City*, 2002 WE Network USA, Bravo Canada, a.k.a. *To Live and Date in New York* 2002 Metro TV, New York, a.k.a. *The Real Sex in the City* 2002 Sky Broadcasting in thirteen countries. Produced by September Films out of London.

[3] *Naked New York with Bob Berkowitz* 2002–2003. 205 episodes. Metro TV, Cablevision, New York.

[4] *New York Moves* 2003–2004 *Dish* Relationship Column

[5] The lead character in HBO's *Sex & the City*, 1998–2004

[6] New York University School of Continuing and Professional Studies 2006–2007, Personal and Life Coaching Certification

behaviors and personality types so you can become a smart shopper. I intend to help you figure out what kind of situation you are currently in, what your personal deal-breakers should be, and how to make your relationships better.

If there is a guy or girl in your life—full-time, part-time, or just wishfully—the following quiz will give you an overview of whether he or she is junk-food, a between-meal snack, or a healthy meal.

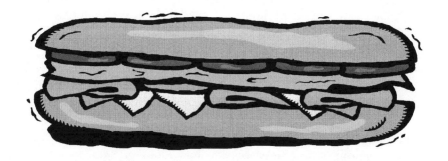

Quiz—Do I Have Junk-Food or a Healthy Meal?

Answer each question below according to how you honestly feel, not with what you believe the right answer should be. Circle the letter that indicates your answer. This quiz is meant for both men and women; just change the pronouns to suit you.

___ 1.) You're making dinner for your guy, and you accidentally leave one of the side dishes in the oven a little too long. What does he do?

A.) He tells me not to worry about it and says that everything else is terrific.

B.) He tells me how I could do it better.

C.) He reminds me about the last time I didn't cook something to perfection.

D.) He yells at me for ruining his dinner and calls me incompetent (or some other name).

___ 2.) You're going to the movies and your girl asks you to find out what time a specific feature is playing. She is late, and when you get there the flick is sold out. How does she respond?

A.) She apologizes for being late and asks if I'd like to do something else instead.

B.) She gives me a bunch of excuses for why she was late.

C.) I apologize and she lets me take the blame.

D.) She blames me for not buying the tickets online and is in a bad mood for the rest of the evening.

___ 3.) You run into an old flame that you haven't seen or spoken to in several years. It's a friendly encounter, but nothing more. How do you handle it with your current meal?

A.) I tell him, and he asks if there is any reason he should be concerned. I assure him there is nothing to worry about, and he thanks me for telling him.

B.) I keep it to myself. He doesn't really ask about what I do.

C.) I tell my guy but then I have to defend myself against his accusatory questions: Did it excite you? What were you wearing? Did you kiss him? Will you see him again?

D.) I can't tell my guy because he'll get crazy and accuse me of cheating on him.

____ 4.) When you're upset about something your girl did, how do you address the situation?

A.) I tell her, and it opens communication to make things better in the future.

B.) I feel comfortable telling her, but he usually gets defensive.

C.) I don't tell her, because it wouldn't make a difference anyway.

D.) If I tell her, it will start an argument. She'll blame me, and I'll end up apologizing to her to calm her down. So I usually just put up with it.

____ 5.) You and your guy are talking to a group of your friends at a party when you casually mention an opinion about something that he doesn't agree with. How does he react?

A.) He says nothing about it in front of my friends but asks to discuss it with me later.

B.) He laughs and rolls his eyes.

C.) He makes an excuse for my ignorance.

D.) He corrects me and tells me to keep quiet.

____ 6.) Which statement best describes your actions in this relationship?

A.) I speak up for what I want while still being thoughtful of her needs.

B.) I mostly just do what I want to do.

C.) I am suspicious. I like to check up on her to see what she's doing.

D.) I walk on eggshells to avoid arguments and keep things going smoothly.

___ 7.) Your family is having a get-together. Your boyfriend has already met them, and he is invited to join you. How does he react?

A.) He is glad to be included and happily go visit my family with me.

B.) He goes, but he is be quiet and moody, making it hard for me to enjoy myself.

C.) He makes a lame excuse for why he can't go or flat-out refuses to be around my family.

D.) He talks me out of going or makes plans to do something I've been wanting to do, making me choose him over my family.

___ 8.) When you disagree about something with your girl, how do you handle the situation?

A.) We calmly discuss it until we reach a compromise.

B.) We yell and argue a bit but usually make up fairly quickly.

C.) She walks out, and I don't hear from her for a while.

D.) She screams at me and manipulates me into doing things her way.

___ 9.) How do your friends and family feel about the way your guy treats you?

A.) They really like him because they can see how happy I am.

B.) They think he's a decent guy, but they hope I'm not planning on getting married to him.

C.) They don't really have an opinion because they haven't spent much (or any) time around us.

D.) They don't like him and keep telling me I could do better. But they don't know him like I do.

____ 10.) How does this relationship make you feel?

    A.) I feel loved, which makes me feel comfortable to love openly. I'm secure and happy. We have a true partnership.

    B.) I'm mostly happy, but we have some problems to work out.

    C.) Frustrated. I love her a lot, but I'm not really happy.

    D.) Alone. I feel like I'm the only one who is trying. I think I love her more than she loves me.

Using the key below, go back and place a value on the score line in front of the number of each question.

A = 5 points

B = 3 point

C = 1 points

D = 0 points

Enter your total score here:

My Total Score _____

If you scored 44–50, you most likely have a well-balanced meal (a serious, long-term relationship). Your choice definitely has potential. This book will aid you in keeping your relationship healthy.

If you scored 36–43, you should consider this relationship a between-meal snack. There are some good qualities here, but he needs to do some work if he wants to become a well-balanced meal. But you can't change him! That will have to be completely up to him. If you're not ready to make a commitment to someone yet, have some fun with him. Use it as practice until you're ready for a well-balanced meal. Just don't place any hope on him becoming one!

If you scored 20–35, you have fast food. Sure, there are healthy bits and pieces if you look hard enough. But you shouldn't have to work that hard. Use this book to modify your palate so you'll welcome healthier meals in the future.

If you scored 0–19, you have junk-food! Dump her. If you're not convinced, the rest of this section will give you specific reasons she's not good for you. You deserve so much better! You seriously need to change your eating habits.

The Junk-Food Ingredient List

Look at the junk-food ingredient list below, and try to determine whether any of these ingredients have been ruining your meals. Place a check mark next to any item that describes your current or most recent partner's actions. Then circle any ingredients that describe your behavior. If you're really honest, you'll be able to figure out how you might be junk-food, too—which is why you're attracting junk-food.

Junk-Food Ingredient List

blame ____	judgment ____
control ____	criticism ____
manipulation ____	verbal abuse ____
jealousy ____	supremacy ____
guilt ____	violence ____
fear ____	lies ____
lack of trust ____	infidelity ____
neediness ____	emotional unavailability ____
competitiveness ____	feelings withholding ____

Next we'll look at how to clearly identify junk-food items and remove them from your shopping list. If you follow the steps recommended in this book, you'll be cooking yourself up a healthy meal in no time.

CHAPTER ONE

The Symptoms of Consuming Junk-Food

I believe a person's happiness level dictates his or her degree of patience and compassion. Think about it. When you're content and life is going well for you, aren't you much more tolerant than when things aren't going exactly as you hoped? If your order takes a little too long, you have to wait in line, or someone bumps into you, it's no big deal, because you have pleasant thoughts running through your head. But how do you respond when you're not entirely happy? Are you easily irritated by another's slowness or mistake? Do you perhaps make nasty comments? Do simple tasks frustrate you? If you find yourself nodding in response to these questions and you're feeling a bit cantankerous and inpatient, that's probably an indicator that you're not entirely happy. If you're in a relationship and you're not happy, you're probably consuming junk-food—or you are junk-food.

As human beings, we are made up of cells, and ours cells produce energy. Some quantum physicists believe our cells *are* energy. Nonetheless, our energy is powerful. It radiates. When a happy, charismatic being enters a room, others take notice—they're drawn to that person. That's because energy is contagious. It makes others feel happy too. But it's not just positive energy that's transmittable. Negative energy is highly infectious. If you're distracted by chemistry and attraction, it's not always easy at first to realize you're being changed. It's usually easier for the people around us to see when someone's not good for us than it is for us to admit it to ourselves. Perhaps someone else even suggested you read this book. If so, that's probably because he or she recognized how much futile energy you're focusing on in trying to make your relationship work. Are you holding on to the fantasy that all the good things that happened in the beginning truly define who your significant other is? Are you hoping he'll change and go back to being the ideal partner you initially saw him to be?

Well, people don't change unless they want to. Most people don't want to. Change is hard. Yet many of us exert too much of our precious time and energy trying to change a lover who doesn't want to change. I know there might be temptation to use this book as a guide to fix your lovable junk-food, but try to resist wasting any more valuable resources on a useless cause. Try focusing all that enthusiasm on fixing yourself! One of my favorite expressions is as follows:

> Nothing changes, if nothing changes.

It's so simple but so true. The only way you can possibly change someone else is by changing yourself, which may in turn change the way he or she responds to you. So, if you are absolutely hell-bent on changing your diamond in the rough, you'll have to start by shifting your focus back to you.

My hope is that this food for thought will incite cravings for healthier choices. I hope to bring you so many epiphanies that you'll never crave junk-food ever again. I promise that if you use this book to refuel and claim your own power, you'll become a magnet for someone fabulous— because energy is contagious. If you are healthy and take care of yourself, you'll naturally attract a healthy partner. But if you stay with someone who is junk-food, you will end up as junk-food too.

This chapter will show you some of the most common relationship spoilers and offer ways to get rid of them for good.

CONSTIPATION—WHEN FEELINGS DON'T FLOW

Experts often say that communication is the essential ingredient of a good relationship. I couldn't agree more! But do you know why? More importantly, do you know how? I'm always disappointed when I hear the way many people in relationships speak to each other after they have gotten comfortable. They sound so disgusted if their partner doesn't do something exactly as they wanted. They bark orders like their spouse is beneath them. I hear it at the mall, in restaurants, and even in church! If that's the way they treat each other in public, what are they like at home? What happened to respect?

What's really going on is more than just a lack of manners. Such behavior usually comes from harbored resentments, unresolved conflicts, and unexpressed feelings. When you hold these things inside and have trouble communicating your needs and desires, you can't help but become irritable. It's just like when you eat a lot of junk food and it binds you up. It's uncomfortable. It makes you sluggish. Sometimes it's even painful. The longer you go without letting things out, the worse it makes you feel.

How do you find relief? Well, people who are constipated as a result of their diet usually eat something healthy, such as beans, bran, or broccoli with garlic. As you might expect, in order to cure a constipated relationship, you need to have lots of healthy communication, as well as a healthy partner. If your partner won't cooperate, then she or he is not the right one! The following quiz will highlight exactly where you need work, whether you're currently in a relationship or not. The pages that follow will help you to create positive change.

Quiz—Does Your Relationship Suffer from Constipation?

Take this quiz twice. The first time, think about your partner and choose the answer that best describes his or her behavior. Circle the letter for your answer. (Or have your partner take it if you think he or she can answer sincerely!) Then go back and take the quiz for yourself; be honest when you choose how you typically react. Write your answers on the "My Choice" lines. Ignore the scores until you're finished. If you don't currently have a partner, answer according to how you would have responded in your last relationship or how you usually handle communication.

____ 1) When I want my partner to do something,

A.) I ask for what I want specifically.

B.) I drop hints about what I want.

C.) I expect my partner to know me inside and out without me having to tell him or her everything I want.

My Choice ____ My Score ____

____ 2) When we have an argument or disagreement,

A.) I'm willing to talk it out until we reach an agreement (even if it's to agree to disagree).

B.) I don't like to be wrong, so I fight to win. I'll say whatever I need to say to get what I want.

C.) I refuse to argue; if saying I don't want to talk about it doesn't work, then I leave.

My Choice ____ My Score ____

____ 3) After we have a discussion or argument about an issue, I

A.) put it behind me and try to uphold any compromises I agreed to.

B.) uphold what I promised for a week or so but then go back to the way things were before.

C.) have a hard time letting it go; I often end up using it as ammunition to reinforce my point in future disagreements.

My Choice ____ My Score ____

____ 4) When my partner tells me his or her concerns about our relationship or something I do that is upsetting,

A.) I listen carefully to what he or she is saying and let him or her finish before responding.

B.) I have a hard time not interrupting to respond to each and every thing as soon as it is said.

C.) I get defensive and usually end up trying to change his or her mind, or I just storm out.

My Choice ____ My Score ____

____ 5) When my partner does something that annoys or upsets me, I usually

A.) tell him or her—in a calm, loving way—how it makes me feel.

B.) snap or make a sarcastic remark.

C.) hold it inside until one day I can't take it anymore, and then I blow up.

My Choice ____ My Score ____

____ 6) When I'm happy about something my partner did and I feel good about the relationship,

A.) I frequently acknowledge his or her positive traits and share my good feelings about our relationship.

B.) I usually say thank you for things he or she does, but I prefer to talk to my best friend about my feelings.

C.) I have a hard time telling my partner what I think and feel.

My Choice ____ My Score ____

____ 7) When my partner shares his or her feelings about me and talks about our future,

A.) I share my true thoughts and feelings too.

B.) I say what I think he or she wants to hear.

C.) it makes me very uncomfortable. I get quiet, stall for more time, or change the subject.

My Choice ____ My Score ____

Using the key below, go back and place a score value on the line in front of the number for each of the choices you made for your partner, and on the My Score line for your choices about yourself.

A = 3 points

B = 1 point

C = 0 points

Enter your total scores here:

His or Her Total Score_____

My Total Score _____

What Your Scores Mean

If you scored 21, you're a healthy communicator! But if your partner scored less than 21, you still have some constipation in your relationship.

If you scored 15–19, you're mostly healthy, but you have a few unhealthy tendencies to give up. If your partner scored low, you might be responding to his or her bad habits.

If you scored 11–14, you're more irregular than regular. You'll find a lot of relief in this chapter.

If you scored 6–10, you have a combination of constipation and diarrhea of the mouth. You shouldn't consume any more food until you digest this chapter.

If you scored 0–5, you're badly constipated! I promise you'll feel much better when you can let your true feelings out. This section is for you!

I hope that you now have an overview of how effectively you communicate your feelings. You should be beginning to see your trouble spots. If your score is high and your partner's is low, your communication needs some help. Try to interest him or her in reading this book.

Communication really does need to go both ways. If he's open to change, he may be a keeper. But if he strongly objects, let it go—and dump him! Trust me; as you get better, you'll want better, and therefore you'll attract better. You are what you meet! (See chapter 7: "Relationship Crash Diet," page 164). When you can figure out why you picked him or her in the first place, then you'll be more likely to pick a healthier meal next time.

If your partner's score is high and your score is low, get your butt in gear or you're going to lose him or her! Obviously, the behavior you both should be striving for is shown in all the "A" answers.

Recipes for Healthy Communication

No Pot Luck Dishes

One of the biggest mistakes in love is expecting your partner to know you so well that he or she will instinctually recognize exactly what you want and need. Is your partner psychic? Does your partner have ESP? No! You shouldn't presume that he or she has such abilities. No matter how intuitive he or she is or how connected the two of you may be, others can never know exactly what you are thinking—unless you tell them. That has nothing to do with how much they love you. More importantly, if you love them, you shouldn't want to put that kind of pressure on them. If you don't express your desires and your partner doesn't get them precisely right, you only have yourself to blame. If you have an expectation, especially if it's important to you, the only way to avoid disappointment and hurt feelings is to share your wishes with your partner. Now, having said that, that doesn't mean you can control what your partner does; all you can do is make the request. It's still up to him or her to decide whether or not to fulfill your request. (You can read about manipulation in chapter 6: "Food Poisoning.")

Oh, and dropping hints isn't enough. Most people don't recognize that a hint is being implied. Even if they do, it's still left up to their interpretation. It's like when someone's cooking something in the next room. Perhaps you smell the tantalizing aroma of garlic. If you're a pasta lover, you might start craving spaghetti and meatballs with garlic bread. But when you walk into the kitchen, you might be disappointed to find a much lighter meal of sautéed vegetables. You got the hint wrong. Hints are ineffective.

Of course, it's no big deal if you guess what's for dinner wrong. But the misinterpretation of thoughts and feelings causes many relationship problems. I recently saw a casual friend of mine whom I haven't seen much since she went through a very nasty divorce. She has three children—the youngest is age nine—and she's a very active mom. She was telling me about a wonderful man she had been dating. He sounded great. Her ex-husband had been verbally abusive, and this guy seemed like his polar opposite—very kind and supportive. (He was handsome too.) I asked why she had stopped seeing him. She said, "He never had children, and he has such an active life. He wouldn't want to take on three kids." "Did he tell you that?" I asked. "Well, no," she said, "I just couldn't see him wanting my life." "Yeah, but you made that decision for him," I said. "Did you ever ask him if he wanted kids?" She looked kind of sheepish as she said no. She started to waver, and I could tell she was considering what I had just said. It seemed to me that she had ended a good thing because of her own insecurity, not for any valid reason.

What if you assume your partner is falling out of love with you or having an affair because she's withdrawn and suddenly unavailable, when the truth is she got fired from her job and had to take a part-time waitress gig until she can find something else and she's just too embarrassed to tell you? Of course she should feel safe to confide in you, but your misinterpretation will most likely add to her stress and potentially ruin your relationship. It will at least drive a wedge between you. It's important not to think you know what your partner is feeling. You have to ask!

You can read more about miscues in the "Heartburn" section of this chapter. The next section deals with unexpressed feelings.

No Pressure Cookers

A pressure cooker works by trapping steam inside, causing the temperature to rise above the boiling point without actually boiling anything. The benefit is that it cooks faster and therefore locks in more nutrients. But when you open the vent to let some of the pressure out, the contents inside will boil. Well, when it comes to communication, there is absolutely no benefit to being a pressure cooker. But it happens all the time.

Let's for a minute think of your feelings as steam. When you keep your emotions inside, withholding your thoughts from your partner, they keep building in temperature—and pressure. Eventually it gets to a point where you just can't conceal any more steam. So when your partner does even the smallest thing that you don't like, you release a little. That starts you boiling, and you might completely blow your top. But it could all be avoided if you would just leave your lid off and openly share your nutrients with your partner.

Sharing your feelings, good or bad, is absolutely crucial to the happiness of your relationship. Again, if your partner doesn't know what's bothering you (or what makes you happy), how can he or she do anything about it? Vice versa, you have to know what's bothering your partner so your imagination doesn't make things worse. I realize it's really hard for some people to talk about their feelings. But if you can create a loving atmosphere, it will get much easier. You have to establish trust. Here are some guidelines to generate a safe environment for communication:

1) Extend an invitation. If you have been snapping at your partner and making sarcastic remarks (emotional ambushing), it's going to be hard for him or her to trust you at first. Buddhists very wisely believe that if you genuinely feel compassion toward another person, there's no way you can be angry with him or her. [7] Try to look at things from your partner's perspective before you take any action.

- Apologize for your previous hostility and tell your partner you want to start over.

- Promise that from now on you'll do your best to treat your partner with compassion.

- Ask to set up an appointed time to sit down and talk.

2) Actively listen.

- Turn off the TV, computer, music, cell phone, and anything else that could interrupt or distract you.

- Say you want to take turns speaking, that you'd like to finish your whole thought before your partner responds, and that you'll offer the same respect to him or her.

- Give your partner your undivided attention.

- Don't look away or around the room.

- Occasionally nod or say "yes" or "uh huh" to let your partner know that you are listening. You can smile if you want when you agree, but don't fold your arms or make dismissive faces when you don't.

- Don't roll your eyes, shake your head, sigh, or laugh sarcastically.

- Keep your body language open. Keep your shoulders square to your partner and sit still. Don't fold your arms or play with your clothes, hair, or jewelry.

- Never assume you know what your partner is going to say; in fact, assume you don't.

- Most importantly, don't plan your rebuttals while your partner is talking. (See the next section, "Diarrhea of the Mouth.") That's how miscommunications occur.

---

[7] Thich Nhat Hanh, *Anger: Wisdom for Cooling the Flames* (New York: Riverhead Books, 2001).

- *Wait your turn, and never interrupt!* You need to hear what your partner has to say.

3) Confirm you understand. When your partner finishes his point, do not respond until you confirm you understand what he meant—especially if you took something personally or it upset you. All too often people get defensive about something that they perceived incorrectly—usually because their own thoughts distracted them from actively listening.

- Put what you heard into your own words and include what you interpreted from your partner's body language. For example: "What I heard you say was ..."

- Don't discount or belittle anything your partner says. Just confirm what you hear.

- Check to make sure you're both perceiving things the same way. (This is called mirroring.) Ask, "Is that what you meant?"

- Take your ego out of it. Be grateful that your partner is sharing his or her feelings. Even if you don't like what he or she is saying, you need to know.

- Think of it as an opportunity to learn about yourself and to grow.

4) Respond compassionately. The goal of any conversation should be to improve your relationship. Keep that in mind when you respond with your feelings.

- Use "I" statements. "I" statements indicate that you take responsibility for your thoughts and emotions.

- Don't blame. "You" statements blame. When you blame, people naturally get defensive, and you'll probably end up arguing.

- It's not about making others wrong; it's about telling them what you need from them.

- Phrase your "I" statements positively, and be specific.

- Don't ever assume you know why your partner did anything or what he or she is feeling.

- Don't make generalized statements using "always" or "never."

26

The last item on that list is especially important. "Always" and "never" imply things about your partner's character rather than his or her specific decisions or actions. These words are character assassins, and they're very hurtful. If you're the kind of person who likes to say whatever will hurt the most in the moment, you should know that one negative statement (attack) will be felt and remembered much longer than one hundred compliments. Phrasing an attack with an "I" statement isn't effective either. The important part is keeping compassion in your delivery. There will be more about this in the section on indigestion. The following chart gives some examples of positive communication:

The Compassionate Way	The Combative Way
"I feel left out when I'm not invited to go out with you and your friends."	"You go out with your friends too much."
"I feel frustrated when you don't take the trash out."	"You forgot to take the trash out again."
"I'd really like it if we could have some romantic dinners with no outside distractions."	"I hate that we eat in front of the TV."
"I feel insecure when you're not open with me."	"I can never get a straight answer from you."
"I've noticed you've been losing your temper more easily. Is there something I'm doing to upset you?	"You always yell at me. What's your problem?"

5) Make amends. First and foremost, apologize for anything you've done that hurt your partner. If that's really hard for you to do, think about this: it's much easier to love you if you show vulnerability than if you show anger. I promise you, it feels much better (and it's much less exhausting) to simply admit you were wrong and say "I'm sorry" than it feels to get all worked up by denying things and defending yourself. *Nobody* is perfect. If you try to be, you'll alienate everyone who tries to get close to you. (See "Silence Your Food Critic" on page 192 for more on perfectionism.)

I wrote these guidelines for communication in numbered and bulleted format to help you see them as a structured conversation. This type of conversation should not be the typical free-for-all you engage in with your friends. It would be helpful for you to start a form of active listening in all conversations. Set a goal to never interrupt anyone. It's a very generous habit to develop that will help all your relationships.

You'll create a loving atmosphere if you choose your words carefully and develop a compassionate delivery. Remember the pressure cooker; you want to prevent steam from building up. As soon as something bothers you, acknowledge it and share it. Your feelings have to flow to keep you from becoming constipated (and irritable). If you always keep your partner's feelings in mind, then you'll speak to her in a kind voice. Energy is contagious. If you're nice to her, she'll most likely be good to you in return. But if she's still not nice to you—dump her! She's junk-food.

Diarrhea of the Mouth

One of the most frustrating things to come up against in a discussion or disagreement is someone who frequently interrupts. Isn't it annoying when you can't finish speaking your thoughts, let alone complete a full sentence? It's called conversation hijacking. It clearly demonstrates a lack of interest. One of the simplest ways to show people you care about them is to listen when they speak. But for many people that's easier said than done. The next time you're with some female friends, notice how often you interrupt each other. You'll do it to add a thought to someone else's, agree with her, or add your experience on the subject she's talking about. It happens all the time, but it's incredibly rude. It says that you don't really care about what the other person is saying; that you just want to talk about you. While you're talking about you, or thinking about what you want to say next, you're missing what she's saying—or trying to say. You're not listening. You're frustrating the speaker.

Unfortunately, this happens so much that it has become a very accepted form of communication. It regularly occurs on TV. Have you ever been watching an interview or talk show when the host has interrupted something you really wanted to hear? Kathy Lee Gifford and the ladies of *The View* do it all the time. Kathy Lee usually does it to be funny. I have to admit that she does make me laugh, but there are times I'm disappointed I didn't hear more of what the guest had to say.

On *The View*, Barbara Walters is great about going back to what guests begin to say. In an episode featuring Dr. Oz, Dr. Oz said, "My wife inspired me to—" Joy Behar then cut him off to ask about something else. He politely answered her. Barbara Walters then interjected: "You were saying your wife inspired you?" He seemed happy that he got to go back to that topic. I thought it was important too. He said that as a heart surgeon, he used to help only those people who came to him after developing heart problems. His wife pointed out that TV could help him take his message to people where they lived so he could help them before they developed heart problems. Barbara Walters is an excellent journalist; she knows it's important to hear what others have to say. That's how you learn new things. In my personal life, I try to always allow others to get their thoughts across. I suggest you try it as well.

When you interrupt your partner in a relationship, it prevents you from resolving issues and getting your needs met. Most people will just shut down and stop trying if they feel like you're not listening anyway—especially if it's not easy for them to share their feelings. Please don't hijack conversations!

If you're too angry or worked up to be able to listen to what your partner is saying, ask to take a break until you can calm down. What really happens while you're taking that break is that a different, less reactionary part of your brain has time to kick in and handle things more reasonably. The best way to force yourself to really listen to what someone is saying is to repeat it back to them in your own words when they're finished. Don't even try to think of a response yet; the desire to respond is what motivates rude interruptions. Put all your attention on listening actively. Then only after you fully comprehend what has been said to you can you start to reply.

Compliments to the Chef

Acknowledgment is one of the greatest gifts you can give. I'm often amazed at how genuinely touched some clients are when I acknowledge them for things they've accomplished, particularly when I point out the positive in something they felt they didn't do correctly. Most of us are used to being told about the negative aspects of things we didn't do right. Our own internal critics are usually the loudest of all complainers. Doesn't it feel great when someone truly compliments you or recognizes your efforts? It makes you feel valued. It raises your self-esteem. When it comes from someone you care about, it makes you feel loved. I once dated a man who had just come out of a long-term abusive relationship. I naturally took to calling him handsome and sexy, as I saw him to be. He seemed taken off guard. He asked me, "Is that what you're going to call me?" I said, "I don't have to if it bothers you." "No," he said, "I like it. I'm just not used to it." His previous girlfriend had frequently called him "loser" and other mean names. The contrast was a little overwhelming for him at first—but in a good way. I could tell I was making him happy.

Giving acknowledgment isn't just for the benefit of the receiver; it's also good for you and your relationship. As you tell your partner things you like about him, you strengthen your affection for him. You can't help but feel great. You're creating positive energy, as well as making your relationship a friendly and safe environment. Every time you think a nice thought about your partner, tell him! He will definitely appreciate it. He may even start doing the same for you.

Now, if giving a compliment is something that's hard for you, perhaps you could start by writing something down. Write a good old-fashioned love letter, or simply make a list of all the things you like about your partner. Then read it every day. Many of us direct our focus to the negative—what's wrong—instead of what's right. Every time one of my clients makes a negative statement, I ask him or her to rephrase it as a positive statement. For example, "He hardly ever takes me out to dinner anymore" could be changed to "We've been eating home a lot to save money, so it's a real treat when we go out." It's the classic glass-half-full-or-half-empty situation. Start noticing the thoughts that run through your head. When you catch a negative thought, rethink it positively. Our thoughts create our feelings, and our feelings create our actions. so think positive thoughts and you'll naturally feel great, which will cause you to react better toward your partner.

I do want to point out that I'm not talking about being phony. If you don't genuinely feel something, don't say you do. It will make you appear untrustworthy. Acknowledgment is much more than just paying a compliment. It's about validating who someone is. Try to be specific with your acknowledgments; they'll mean more that way. Instead of just saying, "You're thoughtful," identify exactly how the person in question was thoughtful and why you appreciate it.

Sharing Your Filling

Emotional intimacy is about feeling safe to be who you are, while allowing your partner to be who she is. It's about creating trust, honesty, and openness. It's what makes couples close. It's the key to true romantic bliss. But sadly, many relationships don't have it. Without it, your liaisons are doomed to fail.

Revealing your true feelings to someone you love can be incredibly rewarding, for some people that's a terrifying thought. Such people think, "What if he rejects me?" or "What if she laughs, or disagrees?" If you are one of those people who have been avoiding revealing their true feelings their whole life, you probably have no idea how to even begin to do so.

Emotional intimacy starts with knowing what you feel. You can't share your innermost emotions until you know exactly what they are. Try writing in a personal journal. Find a quiet place where you won't be interrupted. Start with "Today I feel" and let whatever comes to mind flow onto the page. Don't worry about noting what happened that day; just focus on what you think about it. Once your feelings are clear to you, you'll find it easier to express them to your partner.

True intimacy can only develop in an environment of love and compassion. If you've been fighting and criticizing each other, you need to address those communication problems first. A good start toward emotional intimacy is to do the actions recommended below and pay close attention to chapter 2, "Emotional Anorexia."

Checklist for Relieving Constipation:

✓Three times a week (at least) tell your partner something you really like or love about him. Always show appreciation for things he does for you, no matter how small. A gentle touch, a smile, and a genuine "thank you" mean a lot.

✓As soon as something bothers you, acknowledge it. Ask to schedule a time that's convenient for both of you to talk. In a calm, loving voice, use "I" statements to express your thoughts. Take responsibility for your own feelings, and listen carefully to your partner's. Don't interrupt!

✓Think and act positively. Monitor your thoughts and rephrase anything negative as a positive.

✓If you want something, ask for it specifically.

✓Write your thoughts and feelings in a personal journal at least twice a week.

Bruce Logan

INDIGESTION—

BLAMING, NAGGING, JUDGING, AND CRITICIZING

You know that uncomfortable feeling you get in your stomach when something just isn't right? You can get it from food if you eat too fast or too much, or if you eat the wrong thing. You can also get it by eating while you're upset or stressed. We've probably all experienced indigestion after a meal at one time or another, and it usually isn't something to worry about. You can typically take an antacid and it goes away. But what if that nauseating feeling wasn't caused by food? When your partner hurts your feelings, doesn't that make you feel a little sick to your stomach? It can even make you feel like you want to throw up. Well, just as with food, an occasional occurrence of relationship indigestion is fairly normal. But chronic indigestion is usually the sign of an underlying, more serious problem. With junk-food relationships it's the exact same diagnosis; however, it usually goes unrecognized—and therefore untreated.

If you find that a certain food gives you indigestion, you most likely try to avoid eating it, right? But how about if that hot guy or girl keeps causing you indigestion? Do you turn him or her down, or do you keep going back for more? If more than 10 percent of the time your partner makes you feel upset, stressed, uneasy, or like you've been punched in the stomach, you're suffering from chronic relationship indigestion. This section is intended to help you recognize the symptoms and provide some virtual antacid relief.

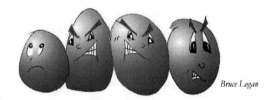

Bruce Logan

Sour Grapes

Verbal abuse is the most commonly ignored form of abuse. Women and men put up with it all the time—mostly because they're unaware of the signs. It can sneak up on you. At first you may make excuses to rationalize bad behavior: "Oh, he just had a hard day." Or worse, you may blame yourself: "I should have known she wanted me to do that." It slowly breaks down your self-esteem. It makes you question yourself and lose confidence, and it can even make you physically sick. But if you can catch it early, it is easy to get away from. Following are some characteristics of verbal abuse.

Criticism: It's abusive if your partner criticizes things you say, how you do things, or what you look like. That may sound obvious, but if she's disguising it as humor, it's harder to recognize—and to stop. If you do rebut her comments, she'll probably tell you you're too sensitive or have no sense of humor. But it's not funny if your feelings are hurt. If she hits on something you already feel insecure about, you may just think she's being honest. Don't rationalize it by assuming she's trying to help you. Did you ask for her help? Or for her opinion? Then she shouldn't give it! Don't allow her to put you down for anything or in any way. She should make you feel valued, not demeaned. A person who criticizes is looking for perfection. No matter how hard you try, you'll never be good enough, because it is impossible to be perfect. If there is something she thinks she could help you do better, she should ask for your permission to make a gentle suggestion. In doing so, it's much nicer if she first compliments the things you do well. But watch out for backhanded compliments that ultimately insult you, such as, "You look good for someone who never works out"—that's passive aggressive.

Judgment: It's abusive if he calls you derogatory names, belittles you for who you are, or ridicules what you believe in, especially if his tone is angry or he yells at you. When you try to defend yourself, he'll probably tell you you're too sensitive and that you should just get over it. He might be passive aggressive by making you the object of his jokes and then trying to convince you that you have no sense of humor when you don't laugh. If you feel as though you've been punched in the stomach while everyone else is laughing, it's not you; it's him—he's junk-food! It's abusive if he disrespects you or humiliates you in front of others.

Blame: It's abusive if she blames you for everything (even if you are at fault). As you'll learn in chapter 7, you have to take responsibility for yourself to make a relationship work. If your partner blames you for anything that doesn't go right, no matter how small, she's probably the defensive type who can't take responsibility for her own actions. She'll always name someone else as the cause for things that happen to her, or have some excuse. She'll never agree that she has any kind of issues (everyone does), so she'll always expect you to do the changing. It's also abusive if she blames you for her feelings of jealousy. If she verbally assaults you every time another woman even glances at you, or gives you the third degree when you go out without her, she's junk-food.

See chapter 6, "Food Poisoning," for more on verbal abuse.

Preventing Indigestion

Table Manners

Don't be a hater. If you can't say anything nice, don't say anything at all. A major cause of indigestion is not putting squabbles and resentments to rest. You need to forgive or get out! Nagging will never help you. Consistently throwing past events in your partner's face can only produce negative results. If you engage in this sort of behavior, you will actually be destroying any love he feels for you. You'll be making yourself the enemy. He'll stop trusting you, and he won't feel safe to tell you any of his feelings. If you cannot truly forgive him and move forward, then you need to leave him. Berating him and harboring negative feelings will punish *you* much more than it will punish him. Plus it will make you into junk-food.

I think the adage "Forgive and forget" is well-intended but a little misleading. I'd prefer you forgive and move forward. If you forget, that might mean you didn't grow from the experience, and you'll most likely go right back to doing things the same way that got you in the argument in the first place.

The way to get closer through disagreements is to respect your partner's wishes when you learn something about his feelings. This shows him you care about his happiness. Sometimes just becoming aware of a desired new behavior is enough to initiate change. But other times, even with the best intentions, bad habits slowly creep back into the relationship. The best way to break a habit is to replace it with a new behavior. Don't just say, "I won't do that anymore"; say, "Instead of doing that, I'm going to do this." For example, if it bothers your partner that you're always late (which bothers most men), decide you're going to be fifteen minutes early for everything. Then if you are a bit late, you'll still be on time.

Food Fights

Do you want to be right, or do you want to be happy? Ask yourself that the next time you find yourself digging in your heels in an argument. What are you really trying to get? Too many of us get caught up in the fight of needing to win, which translates into not wanting to be wrong. But at what cost?

It's impossible to avoid conflicts when two people spend significant amounts of time together. Arguments can actually be good for a relationship; that's how most issues get attention—and therefore resolution. However, the way you handle disagreements can make or break the relationship. If you do it right, they can bring you closer. If you fight to win, you'll ultimately lose. If time and again you turn and run away, you'll never resolve anything, leaving you with constant indigestion.

Sometimes the only solution is to agree to disagree. The objective for any argument should be to find a better way to coexist harmoniously. What gets in the way is our perception. No two brains perceive things the same way, not even in identical twins. [8] So you and I could look at the exact same thing, but see it completely differently. There's no right or wrong; it's just your perception. So sometimes in a relationship you'll have a disagreement about something you simply perceive differently. If you reach an impasse on an issue, check to make sure each of you truly understands the other's point of view. Say, "What I hear you saying is …" (put it into your own words), and then ask, "Is that what you meant?" I think you'll find that frequently the thing you heard was not what she meant, and you can clear up the misunderstanding right then. If you comprehend each other but still prefer it your own way, agree to disagree. That means finding a way to comfortably live with the situation. If you can't, it has to be a relationship deal-breaker.

---

[8] Daniel Goleman, *Emotional intelligence: Why it can matter more than IQ*, 10th anniversary ed. (New York: Bantam Books, 2005).

Bruce Logan

Rules for a Healthy Food Fight

1) **When you feel enraged, don't say anything!** Take a few deep breaths and slowly count to five. It will give the more reasoning part of your brain time to kick in. Listen to it! If you can't control your temper, then tell your partner you need to take a break so you can calm down. Take a walk around the block or postpone the conversation until another day when you can respond rationally.

2) **Never say mean and hurtful things in a moment of anger.** You can say a thousand nice things, but a single insult will be remembered forever. Once it's said, you can never take it back. True love means never wanting to hurt your partner!

3) **Never use sensitive and personal information as ammunition.** It's a violation of emotional intimacy. Things that your partner shared with you in a loving, tender moment have no place in a fight. That's hitting below the belt and a sure way to lose your partner's trust—perhaps even turn him or her against you.

4) **Don't bring up any past issues.** The past is in the past; learn from it and move on. If you can't agree on or make a compromise over a specific issue that isn't a relationship deal-breaker, then you need to agree to disagree. That means you

respect each other's position (and boundaries) and accept what it is. Then put it to rest. Do not bring it up again unless it's to tell your partner you've changed your mind and you now agree. Relationships have to advance; otherwise, they die. Keep your relationship in the present and growing forward.

5) **Fight for happiness, not to be right.** The only winner of a fight should be your relationship. It's much easier to say "I'm sorry" than it is to defend yourself. It's also more endearing. You're much more lovable when you accept responsibility for your actions and be humble. Your goal is not just to make yourself happy, but to also make your partner happy. It will make your relationship better.

6) **You never get nagging rights.** You have to forgive or get out. If he did something (or won't do something) that you can't get past, then you have to leave the relationship. You cannot beat him up about it if you choose to stay. You have to forgive and move forward or successfully agree to disagree.

7) **Don't suppress your anger.** Depression is anger turned inward. You have to express your anger to relieve it and feel better. If you hold everything inside, you become a potential pressure cooker. The anger will build until you ultimately explode on your unsuspecting partner. Or you'll make yourself sick. You'll become passive-aggressive (meaning that though your words seem friendly, your actions are not). Use your communication tools to let your partner know what's making you angry. She can't help you if she doesn't know what it is.

By using the rules above, you can maintain harmony even through tough times. It's all about having compassion. If you truly value your partner's feelings and well-being, then you'll never intentionally hurt him. If you argue lovingly, you can increase emotional intimacy and create a lifelong bond.

But if you or your partner are unable to follow these guidelines, or you find yourselves fighting all the time, then you're probably not a good match. If you have a hard time controlling your anger, then it's an issue for you. A partner who will engage you in arguments will ultimately be very bad for you. Make that a personal junk-food flag. You'll find much more peace with a partner who doesn't like to fight and will not provoke your issues.

Cooking with Fire

Your thoughts, emotions, and actions are your power. Maintaining and using your power properly is the key to finding and keeping a happy, healthy relationship. But power is most frequently defined as control. Control can be a very destructive element in relationships.

There are two ways power is used negatively. The first is through trying to control others. The second is by giving control to others. One of these two scenarios is the primary cause of indigestion in relationships. It's usually subconscious. Until you recognize and make a conscious effort to change your use of your power, your relationships will continue to fail. The good news is that you have the power! You can change your situation without needing anything from anyone else. When you truly accept that the only person you can and need to change is you, you'll find happiness. You can read more about maintaining your power in chapter 7, "Relationship Crash Diet."

Checklist for Relieving Indigestion:

- ✓ If you are in a verbally abusive relationship, get out immediately. You'll find help in chapter 6, "Food Poisoning."

- ✓ Start taking notice of anything you blame someone else for, and find your own responsibility for it instead.

- ✓ Don't be a nagger. If something is bothering you, use good communication and "I" statements to express your feelings.

- ✓ If you've been fighting with your partner, make a peace treaty to always act with compassion. [9] Share the fair fight rules and make a pact to both follow them. Write your peace treaty on paper and both sign it.

---

[9] Thich Nhat Hanh, *Anger: Wisdom for Cooling the Flames* (New York: Riverhead Books, 2001).

Bruce Logan

HEARTBURN—

CHEATING, JEALOUSY, AND INSECURITY

Have you ever had your heart broken? I believe that is a defining question. Post-heartbreak, many of my clients experiencing it for the first time have had epiphanies. All of a sudden, they felt sorry for how they behaved or for things they had said to past lovers before they knew what it felt like to be heartbroken. They didn't previously understand how truly painful their seemingly normal actions were to their exes. Preheartbreak, they weren't capable of such compassion. It's been my experience, both professionally and personally, that preheartbreak, most people are primarily selfish. Those whose hearts have never been broken simply don't have as much emotional depth as someone who has endured heart wounds that brought him or her wisdom.

So it's kind of a catch-22. It sucks to have your heart broken. But at the same time, it's quite possibly the best thing to ever happen to you. I believe it's truly difficult to maintain a healthy, long-term relationship if you haven't had your heart broken. Yet the way your heart breaks will also influence your future relationships. When one person falls in love but the other doesn't, there is heartbreak. That's natural and, for the most part, unavoidable. As long as both people were honest, there shouldn't be any hard feelings, just sadness and possibly the lost hope of having found a good connection. But when one person is deceitful or unfaithful, or if he or she betrays the other, heartbreak becomes heartburn. Heartburn is much harder to get over. It can make you feel angry, insecure, jealous, or bitter. It challenges your ability to trust. But heartburn is frequently avoidable.

When my clients end a relationship, whether a good or bad one, they often ask me if there was something they should have seen in the beginning. The answer is always yes. As they tell me more about how it started, we usually do discover the warning signs that could have prevented their heartbreak. But they had been too caught up in the seduction to pay attention. Frequently they didn't even know what to look for in the first place.

I'm guessing that since you're reading this book, you probably have had your heart broken, or you're at least frustrated with the way things are currently going. If that is indeed the case, I'm well aware that you don't feel that this could actually be good for you. You probably feel that if the one you love would just act lovingly again, you'd be fine. But it doesn't work that way. What you need to do is use this painful experience to empower you. Look for the lessons. Contemplate this: no one can break your heart without your permission. What does that mean? If you don't want someone then they can't break your heart. You need to be smart about whom you allow yourself to love. Despite any attraction you may feel, you have to realistically assess their junk-food potential—before you allow yourself to fall in love. Knowledge is your best protection.

Read the Ingredients

First and foremost, when your new sweetheart tells you something about himself, believe him! I can't stress this enough. If he says, "I'm not ready for a serious relationship," don't think, "Well, maybe not with anyone else, but you have such a great connection with me." The connection part may be true—but it doesn't change the fact that he's not ready for more. If you ignore that important ingredient, you will get hurt. I had a client who came to me devastated because his girlfriend had cheated on him. But she had told him in the beginning that she had never been faithful to anyone. He trusted the connection he felt and assumed he'd be different, instead of truly hearing what she said. That was a painful mistake. She ultimately did what she said she would do. When people talk about themselves, it's not in relation to you. It probably has nothing to do with you; it's all about them. You can't change them. You have to accept their truth!

It might not be that blatant, but people will always reveal themselves if you're paying attention. One client said to me after a long discussion about her man's unavailability, "Well, he did make a joke that he was commitmentphobic." Humor is based on truth. When others try to disguise an issue by making light of it, take it as a fact. Most people do know on some level what their shortcomings or issues are. Your partner may say, "I'm a lousy boyfriend," Meaning "I'm not good at relationships; don't get too attached to me, as I will never make a true commitment." She may say, "Kids are ballbusters" or "Kids are a lot of work," which translates to "I will never have kids." If your partner says something like this out loud to you, then his or her conscience will be clear when it doesn't work out. Your partner told you; it's up to you to listen.

A client of mine was in love with a man who told her he just wanted to be "friends with benefits." She told him that didn't work for her and that she needed more. But then she continued to see him. She thought that since she had told him that didn't work, he was agreeing to her terms. But in reality, by continuing to see him, she was agreeing to his terms. He didn't say, "Okay, I'll give you a commitment." In fact, he said, "I'm not good at relationships." She then said, "Why don't you let me be the judge of that." So he continued to call. In his mind, he had established that they were only friends with benefits. She continued to be frustrated with his sporadic availability. I told her that if she wanted to have more from him, she had to stop seeing him. He had no incentive to give her more, because he was getting what he wanted. People do what they want to do. If he wanted to see her after she cut him off, he would have to meet her on her terms. If he never came back, then she would have saved herself potential years of heartburn. While you're pining for a junk-food relationship, you have no possibility of finding a healthy meal. Don't allow your love cravings to leave you in limbo.

Since I started by speaking of those who had never suffered a broken heart, let me caution you that if your partner has never had his or her heart broken, you should guard yours. When you ask your partner if she has suffered heartbreak, if she has to think about it or says something like "I guess so," then she has not suffered true heartbreak. Having your heart truly broken is not something you forget or have to take time to recall. It's a life-altering experience that stays with you. Not getting your way is not the same thing as having your heart ripped apart. If your partner has not truly had his heart broken, that doesn't mean that he is not capable of being a keeper. But if something goes wrong, he will most likely bail out quickly. Without the depth and compassion that develops through experiencing emotional pain and adversity, people are usually self-absorbed. They may not intend to be selfish; they're just unaware of any other way. They don't truly know themselves. Everyone has issues that need to be healed in order to sustain a healthy relationship. But most people don't know what their sabotaging issues are until something or someone stimulates them. Those who have never suffered heartbreak are usually less willing to work on, or even acknowledge, their issues when they come up. Most of the time they'll blame you for the anxiety or uneasiness that they're feeling. Subsequently, they are frequently the ones who cause you the most heartburn—usually because you don't see it coming. In most cases, neither did they.

Another caution: if your meal says "People don't change," that means he or she will probably never change. People have to want to change, and even then it takes motivated work to achieve growth. Someone who has never wanted to change, and therefore hasn't experienced much change, will frequently believe that change isn't even possible. This person may also express negative opinions about therapy or simply question its purpose. All this means that when problems arise in your relationship, your partner is not going to be willing to change anything. He will most likely blame you for not loving him the way he is. I think it's cowardly to expect anyone else to change while you stay the same.

The Recipe

You have to live in the present. Put your attention on what is immediately in front of you and take it at face value. Your imagination is not your friend in relationships. You've probably already heard that you're not supposed to start fantasizing about the wedding as soon as you meet a great catch. If you haven't, you're hearing it now. As you start to see more of each other and your feelings begin to deepen, it's imperative to remain in the present. If you start imagining the relationship to be more than it is, you'll throw it off balance. You may impose unrealistic expectations. You may loosen your boundaries and open yourself to potential heartbreak—overlooking any junk-food flags. If you misinterpret your partner's behavior to be something that it's not, your partner may think you're crazy or high-maintenance. Neither is good.

The most destructive way your imagination misbehaves is by trying to read into your mate's behavior. Even if you're psychic, or if you have ESP or a PhD in psychology, you don't know what he's thinking or feeling unless he tells you. Stop driving yourself and the person in your life crazy! I've seen too many people, especially girls, freak out on good partners because of some imaginary scenario they've been playing out in their head. This type of behavior usually comes from insecurity or neediness. It's drama. That's a major junk-food flag to a well-balanced meal.

When you catch yourself getting all worked up and calling your friends to complain about something you think is going on with your man, stop! Ask yourself what the facts are. Only respond to what is *actually* going on, not what you *think* is happening. Do not decide what *he* is thinking. Most of the time you'll be wrong and you'll risk damaging the relationship.

You have to be careful about the intentions and baggage of your friends, too. They may mean well (or sometimes not), but their insecurities can increase yours and can put ideas in your head that will cause you to alienate your partner. I've seen that happen all too often. If you're questioning something in your relationship and you need to talk to someone about it, try to get more than one friend's opinion. Stick to the facts by describing the situation with as little drama as possible. Don't inject your opinions, emotions, or what anyone else thinks. Choose to confide in people who have happy relationships if you can. Be very wary of friends who fuel your fire. Venting actually perpetuates your thoughts; it doesn't release them.[10] The role of a good friend should be to help you see a situation more clearly, not make it worse.

Now, I do feel I should point out that there can be a fine line between trusting your instincts—which I definitely recommend—and creating a situation that doesn't exist. You need to know yourself and be in touch with your inner feelings. The recipes in this book are intended to help you sort out your own ingredients too.

---

[10] John J. Ratey and Albert M. Galaburda, *A User's Guide to the Brain: Perception, Attention, and the Four Theaters of the Brain* (New York: Pantheon Books, 2001).

Food Envy

It's been said that it's not *love* that's blind, but jealousy. When left unbridled, jealousy is an incredibly destructive emotion. But if you give jealousy vision, you can use it as an insightful tool to determine the quality of your relationship.

Jealousy has several different characterizations, but at its core, there's usually insecurity. It's natural to feel a little jealous at the beginning of a significant relationship. Actually, it's a good sign. If you're not jealous, then you don't really care, right? As those amorous feelings start to develop, you're generally not yet assured of some very important elements, such as whether or not she returns your feelings, wants the same things, or deserves your trust. You're vulnerable. Hence, a little jealousy sparked by past lovers or a stranger flirting with your meal is completely justified. If she acts a little jealous too, she probably does return your feelings. But as the relationship progresses and real trust is earned—and that takes time—the jealousy should be replaced by security. If it isn't, then jealousy becomes a warning sign.

Once you're in an established, committed relationship, if you're so jealous that you make sarcastic remarks or start an argument anytime another man or woman is mentioned (even a coworker or family member), or you keep a watchful eye over everything your meal does, you need to do some soul searching. Ask yourself if you're being realistic. Does your partner give you reason to suspect her of cheating? Has her behavior changed? If you can honestly answer yes, or if this jealous behavior is completely out of character for you, then trust your instincts; she probably is being dishonest. Don't allow her to justify bad behavior, make you feel crazy, or blame you for her actions (after all, the best defense is a good offense). When you maintain your power, you command respect. If she or he doesn't inspire you to feel loved and secure—get out now! Without trust, it isn't a real partnership anyway. But you have to be absolutely honest with yourself. If you can admit that your jealousy isn't motivated by your meal's actions, then you need to do some healing before you ruin the relationship you're so afraid of losing.

I have a client I'll call Melissa, who is a very jealous woman. She has been dating a wonderful well-balanced meal named Greg for over a year now. He has proven himself to be faithful, supportive, trustworthy, and very patient. Yet I spend hours on the phone with Melissa every month (sometimes every week) trying to calm her anxiety and help her see how her imagination is her only problem. She's her own worst enemy because she's perpetually unhappy in a relationship most women would feel very secure in. The good news is that she recognizes that the problem is her. Melissa's frequent calls to me are made to prevent her from freaking out on Greg unnecessarily, thus ruining her relationship. The bad news is that she hasn't successfully overcome her insecurities yet.

Greg is heavily involved in philanthropy, which consequently has him working with a lot of women. He also takes a class at the gym every week that is taught and attended by women. He invites Melissa to do all these things with him. She has gone, but she doesn't really like it. Her perception is that these women want her man. She interprets his friendly personality as a threat, because other women are always friendly in return to him. She sees that as flirting. I ask her if she feels Greg is being disrespectful or giving her cause to think he'd ever be unfaithful. She says, "No, he's great. It's the women who are being disrespectful; they're not friendly to me." But she's not friendly to them either. In fact, she's usually fuming inside that she even has to be there with them in the first place. I suggested that perhaps the women sense that she doesn't like them, so they just leave her alone. I've tried to encourage her to make friends with them to ease the tension. Melissa can see my point, but that doesn't help dissuade her conviction that the women are all scheming temptresses. She just wants Greg to stop taking the class, but there is no valid reason for her to make that request. He really enjoys it. I've suggested that she stop going. Then she stays home and worries about what's happening without her there to keep an eye on things. Either way, she's unhappy. She feels exactly the same about his charity events too.

One day, Melissa called me very upset because Greg was going to attend a four-day conference nearby with several women from work. She wanted to go with him, but he told her tickets were expensive and he couldn't afford to take her. There was a welcome party intended for spouses that he had already invited her to. That wasn't good enough for Melissa. She called the organizer and manipulated her way into a free press pass to attend the entire event. She was proud of herself for her innovation. I was a little horrified. That was a bold violation of Greg's boundaries. I asked what Greg said when she told him she had gotten the ticket. She said he didn't seem to mind, but he didn't offer to take her with him. That's why she was upset. She wanted me to help her figure out how to get him to tell his coworkers he couldn't drive them. She was trying to rearrange his entire itinerary to accommodate her. I reminded her that it was his work and that she needed to trust him and allow him to do whatever he felt was best for his job without interfering.

Melissa's real problem is that she doesn't truly believe in herself. She doesn't see herself as a great catch. There is a big part of her that doesn't understand what Greg sees in her, which is why she feels threatened by other women. It doesn't help that she has no hobbies or interests of her own. On top of that, she only works part-time. She has too much idle time on her hands and not much to focus her thoughts on besides her relationship. On the other hand, Greg works full time, chairs several charities, and works out four days a week. He has taken off work to accompany Melissa to medical procedures, taken vacations with her family, and accommodated most of her needs and desires. He's not great at expressing his emotions, which probably perpetuates Melissa's insecurity. But he consistently shows her that he is completely committed to her and their relationship.

With my encouragement, Melissa has started taking some classes to give her something positive to devote her energy to. It's helping to boost her self-esteem. She is also reading *Co-Dependent No More: How to Stop Controlling Others and Start Caring for Yourself* by Melody Beattie. If you can relate to Melissa's story, I highly recommend the same for you. Put your attention on you, and take care of you. A trustworthy partner should give you comfort; if that's not what you're experiencing, you need to make some changes.

Start by trying to pinpoint the source of your insecurity. Perhaps you just don't feel desirable enough. If you've been burned before, you're most likely gun-shy and reacting to your current meal as you did to your ex. Or maybe *you* have a tendency to cheat, in which case you're probably projecting your own behavior on her. Whatever it is, it's not fair. You need to stay in the moment and only react to what's in front of you. You have to stop trying to control anyone else; you can only control yourself. In all probability the thing making you jealous is low self-esteem, just as in Melissa's case. If you don't truly feel lovable, how can you possibly believe or trust anyone who says he or she loves you?

What should your meal's jealousy be saying to you? Of course, a little occasional jealousy can be cute and make you feel loved. But when it becomes obsessive and you start to feel more like a possession than a partner, run! Overly jealous people need to be in control. They won't *allow* you to do things on your own. They'll attack you (verbally or physically) to beat down your self-esteem so you'll think you need them more. Don't fall for it. Maintain your power! Naturally that includes checking in with yourself to make sure you're being honest. Are you causing this jealousy? Are you overly flirtatious? Do you need a lot of attention? Do you have to be the main attraction at a party? I have to tell you, those are not endearing qualities; they're symptoms of low self-esteem.

So jealousy can be good, bad, or even dangerous. (Chapter 6, "Food Poisoning," will help you determine if it's dangerous.) I hope that now, whenever you feel jealousy, you'll open your eyes to what it's saying. In fact, I hope that whenever you feel fearful or insecure, you'll think to ask yourself, "What's really going on?" Learn to accept responsibility for your part in it.

I could devote an entire book to the symptoms and resolutions of every fear that gets in the way of healthy relationships. Chapter 2, "Dating Disorders," will tell you a lot more about fear and how to handle it. But what it all boils down to is loving yourself completely and maintaining your power. You need to build your self-esteem by giving yourself the attention you crave. A good way to start is by doing the following exercise:

Building self-esteem

1. Using a pen or pencil in a notebook or journal, physically write down all your good qualities. Do not type into a computer. Your brain will absorb and connect with the information more effectively if you write it by hand. List in detail what makes you unique, special, and lovable. Embrace your differences; they're good! Include things you'd like to be or have, and write everything in the present tense, as if it is already happening. For example, "I am very creative." Really think about each trait as you list it.

2. On a separate sheet of paper, write down any negative thought that disputes the good things you write about yourself. For example, if while you're writing "I'm lovable" your inner voice is saying "No you're not; John didn't love you," write that

down. Write out whatever you truly feel. Use as many pages as you need.

3. When you're finished, review your negative thoughts. If you were truly honest, you should have a very specific picture of the fears that are invading your relationships. Sometimes just being aware of a problem is enough to change it.

4. On another sheet of paper, write a positive affirmation for each of your negative thoughts. For instance, to counteract the negative example above, write, "I am very lovable to men who are good for me." Write each affirmation ten times by hand, and really think about what you're saying as you write. Write out reasons to support why each affirmation is true.

5. Update your first list with any new positive affirmation you have created. Then, every day, read your list aloud and congratulate yourself for all your wonderful qualities.

6. Do something nice for yourself daily.

Cheating on your Diet

Perhaps the greatest cause of heartburn is the feeling of betrayal. Trust is an essential ingredient of a healthy meal, and once it's lost or threatened, it's extremely hard to get back. Unfortunately, cheating is a part of far too many relationships. As of September 8, 2012, statistics from the Associated Press reported that

- 35% of men and women have professed they cheated while on business trips,

- 74% of men and 68% of women stated they would establish an affair if they knew they could not be discovered,

- 3% of US children are the result of a cheating spouse,

- 57% of men and 54% of women polled stated that they committed the act of

cheating in any relationship they obtained in their lifetime, and

- the average affair lasts two years. [11]

Many of my female clients and also my gay male clients have expressed their belief that all men cheat, either because they have never dated a faithful man or because they're trying to justify being in love with a man who is incapable of being faithful. I say incapable only because they have not chosen to value fidelity—not because of any genetic predisposing. Scientists at the Kinsey Institute came out with a study in recent years noting that one in four individuals is born with a certain variant of the DRD4 gene that makes them more likely to have a history of uncommitted sex, including one-night stands and acts of infidelity. The gene causes a dopamine rush in their brain similar to that of a gambler hitting a win or an alcoholic taking a drink. That information gave many cheaters the backup they needed to condone and validate their desire to cheat, as if they had no control over it. Still other cheaters just use history as their excuse; mistresses have been written into historical records for centuries. Despite how convincing any predisposed claims may be, we as human beings have free will to change anything we want. We can be *anything* that we truly believe we are. Someone with the alcoholism gene can choose not to drink. It may not be easy, but it is possible. Similarly, anyone who has cheated can choose to become faithful; any guy who tries to tell you otherwise is junk-food.

Beyond anyone who may have to try hard to remain faithful, there are a lot of very honorable people who choose to never cheat. They simply don't believe in it. Cheating is a choice, and not all people cheat! If that has never been your experience, then you've been choosing the wrong partners.

There is no failsafe way to know if your meal will cheat on you or not. But there are some signs you can look for in the early stages of dating. Just one of these behaviors on its own may not be cause for alarm, but if you observe three or more, you can safely consider the person in question junk-food.

---

[11] Associated Press, *Journal of Marital and Family Therapy*, research date September 8, 2012, quoted by Statistic Brain at http://www.statisticbrain.com/infidelity-statistics/.

1. **He has an overinflated ego.** He thinks he's perfect and that everyone else should think so too. He's competitive in all that he does and doesn't think the rules apply to him. To him, cheating is a validation of how wonderful he is. Since the rules don't apply to him, he feels free to cheat as he likes.

2. **She has cheated before.** The best predictor of the future is the past. In the beginning of dating, you should ask if she has ever cheated. The way she responds may tell you a lot. If she says she did once but felt horrible afterward, then that's not bad. She probably learned from the experience. If she admits she cheated but blames her partner at the time or has some other excuse, that's a sign that she's capable of cheating on you, too. If she uncomfortably avoids answering the question, take that as a yes; she's a cheater.

3. **One of his parents was a cheater.** We get our paradigm of relationships from our parents' behavior. If one or both of his parents cheated, especially if it was his dad, his core belief is that people cheat. That's not to say that he will definitely cheat. He may have seen how destructive it was and vowed to never cheat himself. If someone your new man loves cheated when he was a child, ask him how he feels about it. Find out if he considers it acceptable behavior.

4. **She's a good liar.** I'm not talking about little white lies to avoid hurting someone's feelings. I mean she easily lies to make herself appear better than she is, or to keep herself out of trouble. If she can lie without conscious she'll have no problem lying to you.

5. **He feels no guilt or remorse.** He doesn't make amends or take responsibility when he has done something wrong or hurts someone. He just shrugs things off as though they mean nothing. He'll have no problem cheating on you.

6. **She's overly sexual and ascribes no deep meaning to sex.** She doesn't make love; it's just sex. If she holds no real value on the feelings that can accompany sex, then it will be no big deal for her to have sex with someone else. Don't mistake passion for feelings. See chapter 3, "Comfort Food Overindulgence."

Once you've been comfortable in your relationship for a while, there are more cheating tells you can look for:

1. **A sudden change in his or her appearance.** He or she starts working out more, buying new clothes, or wearing cologne.

2. **He or she is not as interested in having sex with you** and/or has stopped cuddling with you.

3. **He or she brings you unexpected gifts.** He or she probably feels guilty and is trying to make amends.

4. **She's unavailable.** Suddenly she's working late, running more errands, and doing things that don't include you.

5. **He's picking fights.** He's trying to justify that your relationship isn't working.

6. **She is struggling with moving the relationship forward;** she's not ready to get married or have a baby.

7. **He lost his job.** Most men identify themselves by what they do, so many men who lose their jobs also lose some of their sense of self. An affair can make them feel good about themselves.

8. **She has new habits.** She's ordering a new drink. She doesn't answer her cell phone around you, it's now password protected, and she no longer leaves it sitting out. She used to leave her e-mail open, but now she always closes it. She may even have a new private account.

Burning Yourself

A social media user has easy access to potential heartburn. I've always believed that snooping is a bad idea. If you find something that upsets you in your snooping, you can't ask about it without admitting that you were snooping. Snooping is a major violation of boundaries and is very destructive to the trust in your relationship. Yet if you don't admit you snooped, then you have to live with the heartburn of what you found. I think the nutritious choice is not to snoop. But with the popularity of social media, you can now be invited to snoop in someone's past and present. I know it's not called snooping; however, I feel it holds the same vulnerability. The danger is discovering something that's completely innocent but allowing your insecurity to blow it out of proportion or make it something it's not. Even worse, it gives you too much information that you wouldn't have known any other way. I think there should be a "don't ask, don't tell" policy in the early stages of dating, meaning that until you have an acknowledged commitment, you should both be dating other people, but not necessarily telling the other about it. However, posts, Tweets, and uploads frequently reveal sensitive information that is inappropriate to share in a new relationship.

I can't even tell you how many clients have called me upset about something they read or saw on their lover's social page. One client I'll call Susan didn't call me until *after* she had already freaked out on the guy she was crazy about. She saw a post about him and another girl, and she then called and told him off. He dumped her. When she called me, it was to see if she could get him back. Unfortunately, the damage had already been done. He thought she was crazy. You see, they had only had a few dates, but she had slept with him. They had never said they were exclusive, and Susan hadn't asked if he was seeing anyone else. She caused her own heartburn and ruined any chance of a real relationship. All because she saw something that she shouldn't have.

Susan did two things wrong:

1.) She had sex without asking for a commitment.

2.) She accepted access to information that was none of her business.

Now, one could argue that she saved herself valuable time by finding out he was a cheater. But did she? She has no idea what that other girl's relationship to him is. She might be a friend, a relative, or just a casual date. Susan might have been the girl he was crazy about. But when she attacked him for essentially no reason, it turned him off. (See chapter 3, "Comfort Food Overindulgence," page 90, for more about when to have sex.)

The pattern I see over and over again is social media relaying very important information that is either misconstrued or that comes from the wrong source. The whole "If you see something, say something" campaign does not apply to relationships. Being an open book is a sign of unhealthy boundaries. Be smart about social media. Dating is hard enough; don't sabotage your efforts by causing your own heartburn. If you want to have a social page:

- Don't post anything you wouldn't want dates or lovers to know about.

- Don't snoop on your love interest's or ex-lover's social pages.

- Don't accept invitations or extend invitations to anyone until you're in a committed relationship. Even then, use caution.

One client told me that her boyfriend of two years was getting hit on by strangers who liked his Facebook profile, even though it said he was in a relationship. They both smartly agreed to take down their pages.

The most senseless way social media causes heartburn is after a breakup. The lure to keep tabs on an ex-lover by looking at his or her Facebook page is self-destructive. Clients frequently spend hours on the phone with me combating their anxiety about a picture they saw, or a post they read, that they wouldn't even have to deal with if they didn't look for it. I continually stress to them that they need to stop looking; the only way for them to feel better and move on is to cut all contact and remove all stimulus of the relationship. The common phrase "out of sight out of mind" is very helpful when you're trying to get over someone.

Frequently, exes do unfriend each other, but remain friends with all the people they share in common. Then when they see something upsetting, they end up posting retaliatory items to get back at the other. Don't make excuses to keep nibbling on that sugary cookie. It's playing games, and it can become a painful, silent war. You may feel that it would be rude to unfriend your ex-lover's friends and family, but if keeping contact is hurting you, then you have to put yourself first and cut all contact. You could send a nice note and say you have enjoyed the relationship and appreciated their support, but you need to take care of you and move on. Anyone who truly cares about you will understand.

Eating off of Someone Else's Plate

I do understand the hypnotic anticipation that pulls you toward someone you're highly attracted to. I also understand that getting him or her for your own can be a thrilling challenge if it involves stealing them from another woman or man. But if that's something you endorse, I want you to understand how you're setting up your own heartburn. As we established, the past is the best predictor of the future. So, while you may be absolutely amazing, that doesn't change the other person's belief that monogamy isn't valuable. If that person leaves someone for you, they *will* cheat or leave you for someone else. It's not about you; that person is junk-food. A healthy meal would never break a commitment unethically. If you feel you have the self-esteem to know you are absolutely amazing and can therefore get any meal you want, I have to tell you that violating someone else's boundaries is a sign of low self-esteem. Self-confidence is not the same thing as self-esteem. Self-confidence is your belief in your ability to do things. Self-esteem is your perception of your own worth. Going after a meal who is taken by someone else indicates you don't value yourself enough to want a healthy meal. Perhaps you don't feel you deserve one. That kind of behavior also shows others you don't care about nurturing healthy self-respect.

I find this this statistic from the Associated Press to be particularly disturbing:[12]

> 17% of men and women have implied they cheated with a sister or brother in law.

Ouch! Put yourself in the shoes of the spouse who was cheated on. That's a double betrayal. When I hear stories like that, I can't help but think, "What were you thinking?" But of course I know the cheater was only thinking about himself or herself. That kind of betrayal is about a lot more than self-gratification. Sibling rivalry is undoubtedly a factor. For a junk-food man, it can be the ego boost of getting the notch in his belt for "doing sisters" or "getting my brother's wife." Most married men cheat only for gratification, not to replace their wife. Even if they think that what she doesn't know won't hurt her, *they* know. Secrets are destructive. It's human nature for us to subconsciously create problems that make others wrong, when we know we have wronged them. It helps us feel better about ourselves. Chapter 5, "Forbidden Fruit," will tell you more about cheating with a married man or woman. If everyone had high self-

---

[12] Associated Press, *Journal of Marital and Family Therapy*, research date September 8, 2012, quoted by Statistic Brain at http://www.statisticbrain.com/infidelity-statistics/.

esteem and compassion for other human beings, then cheating could never happen. It boils down to doing unto others as you want them to do unto you. As the saying goes, karma is a bitch. Try not to burn yourself.

Checklist for Relieving Heartburn

✓ Keep your thoughts in the present. Don't let your imagination get carried away. Keep your fantasies in check.

✓ Believe what you are told. You cannot change anyone.

✓ Don't read into behavior. Trust your instincts, but don't create something that's not there.

✓ Be smart about social networking. Less is more.

✓ Look for signs of cheating, and make nutritious choices.

✓ Build your self-esteem.

Doggie Bag
The Symptoms of Consuming Junk-Food

➡ **Nothing changes if nothing changes.** If you are not happy, initiate positive change.

➡ **You can't change or control anyone else.** If you want someone to change, you have to change yourself, which *may* change the way the other person responds to you. If changing yourself doesn't positively change your partner, you have to take care of yourself and walk away.

➡ **Communicate responsibly.** Don't hold feelings and frustrations inside. Calmly share them with your partner. Listen actively—you need to know what your partner has to say.

➡ **Ask for what you want.** No one can give you what you want if he or she doesn't know what you want. Don't assume you know what your partner is thinking or feeling, either. You have to ask.

➡ **Fight to improve your relationship, not to win.** It's impossible to avoid arguments when two people spend a lot of time together and have deep feelings for each other. Just never lose compassion for your partner, and work toward the objective of making things better for both of you—not just you.

➡ **People tell you who they are.** Pay attention, and believe them!

➡ **Jealousy without valid cause is a signal that you need to raise your self-esteem.** Have a busy life of your own and make your primary focus you.

➡ **Be smart about social media.** Enforce a "don't ask, don't tell" policy in the beginning of a relationship. Less is more when it comes to publicly posting personal information. And don't snoop on your potential lover or ex lover's page.

➡ **Once a cheater, always a cheater.** People can change, but only if they want to. Most people don't want to. Ask your partner if he or she has ever cheated. If the answer is yes, be prepared for future heartburn.

CHAPTER 2

Dating Disorders

I believe fear is the root of all relationship problems. The most common fears are fear of abandonment, fear of intimacy, fear of commitment, fear of change, fear of rejection, fear of failure, and even fear of success. Everyone has fear on some level. We develop it in our childhood. As an adult, you have to become skilled at controlling your fears. If you don't, they will surface in your relationships and cause you to act in destructive ways.

If you're afraid your partner doesn't love you as much as you love him, you'll start to act out of insecurity rather than love. You may try to manipulate him into loving you more by using guilt or blame, or by playing the victim. If you're afraid he's going to leave, you may become needy and smothering—hanging on for dear life—or you may begin competing with him to prove your worth. You may start to sabotage the relationship, creating arguments over nothing or acting out. You may become jealous of others that you perceive your partner finds more attractive—which only makes you less appealing. Or you may just keep your thoughts, needs, and desires to yourself because you fear that if he really knew you, he wouldn't love you. All of these actions, conscious or not, drain your energy because they put your happiness in the hands of someone else. When you engage in these actions, you give away all your nutrients.

When you succumb to your fears by taking insecure action, the result is usually what you fear most: you push him away and he leaves you. Alternately, when you act nutritious by choosing to face your fears and to accept responsibility for them, you can gain wisdom to make your relationships better.

Stepping on the Scale

Before you can heal your issues, you have to acknowledge what they are. The best way to discover your obstacles is by taking an honest look at whom you are attracted to and whom you choose as your romantic partners. You may think your attraction depends on how hot, sweet, or successful your partner is. But the psychology behind our romantic choices says our attraction is based on our unresolved childhood wounds.[13] Subconsciously, we choose partners with the same personality traits, and even physicality, of the parent or caretaker we had the most problems with. You might be thinking, "That's ridiculous; I never even got along with my mother, why would I want to date her?" But it's the devil we know, it's comfortable, and subconsciously we're drawn like a magnet to people with similar characteristics. Since we couldn't heal those conflicts as a child, we try to heal them as adults. We do so through our romantic relationships. The problem is that most people don't want to work on their issues. So when they come up in your relationship, they usually tear it apart.

Harville Hendrix, PhD, created what he calls IMAGO therapy.[14] He believes that the best way to heal your childhood issues is by engaging in

---

[13 & 14] Harville Hendrix, *Getting the Love You Want: A Guide for Couples*, 20th anniversary ed. (New York: H. Holt, 2008).

a loving relationship with a partner who stimulates those issues. If you are lucky enough to have a partner who is willing to work on your shared issues, it can be the best relationship you ever had. However, finding that agreeable someone can seem like looking for a needle in a haystack. Remember, you can't change anyone; people have to want to change. I suspect the reason you're reading this book is that you keep finding partners who won't, or don't think they need to, work on any issues. I suggest learning what your issues are and then learning how to identify and avoid the specific traits that don't work for you when you're choosing a partner.

The following exercise is imperative for you if you want to improve your relationship choices. You may think that all your romantic partners have been very different. Perhaps on some level that is true. But if you start to dig deeper, I think you might be surprised at what you find.

What is Your Pattern?

1) Make a list of all your significant romantic partners.

2) Next to each name, list all his qualities and characteristics; include both positive and negative traits. For example: giving, affectionate, trustworthy, judgmental, argumentative, controlling, cheap, jealous, emotionally closed, selfish, generous, etc. Be as specific as you can.

3) On a separate page, list the primary caretakers from your childhood. Include older siblings and any close relatives.

4) List all the qualities and characteristics of each family member.

5) Compare your two lists side by side. Highlight all the characteristics your people have in common.

6) Draw a circle around the family member that has the most personality traits in common with the people you've dated.

You'll most likely discover that the meals you've been choosing share personality traits with one of your caretakers. It won't necessarily be the parent of the opposite sex; it's usually the person you argued with, couldn't communicate with, or were forced to be the adult for, the one who you never felt good enough for, or the one you never got enough time with. Possibly even all of the above.

What Are Your Personal Junk-Food Flags?

Now that you have a list of all the qualities and characteristics that don't work for you, use them as your own personal junk-food flags to watch out for. If you've dated a lot of controlling meals because your mother was controlling, then you now know you have to avoid controlling meals in the future. If your mother never said, "I love you," you've probably been dating emotionally unavailable meals. Now that you've done this exercise, when you feel incredibly attracted to someone who has your mother's difficult yet familiar qualities, you should be able to stop and say, "Oh no. Been there, done that—this doesn't work for me!" This way you won't waste another day of your precious time on the wrong person. No matter how attracted you are, you'll know that he or she is not good for you. Don't go there! It may be hard for you to avoid the wrong people at first, but as it really sinks in that those kinds of meals won't make you happy, you'll find yourself genuinely attracted to healthier partners.

What Are Your Personal Healthy-Meal Flags?

After you've finished the pattern exercise, go back and make a third list of all the positive character traits that do work for you. Add any that you know you'd like but haven't experienced yet. Use those qualities as healthy-meal flags when you see them in a potential partner. Your list of personal junk-food flags, combined with your healthy-meal flags, make up the requirements that you need to have for a happy relationship. Now that you have a better idea of what does and does not make you happy, you should be able to make better choices in romantic partners.

Everyone has some issues; remember, nobody is perfect. You have to find someone who has his or her issues under control, or whose issues don't stimulate your issues negatively. Then respect each other by not intentionally pushing known emotional buttons.

Just as healthy food tastes different than junk food, healthy relationships feel different than unhealthy relationships. Junk food tastes better? Well, maybe at first, but after adjusting to a healthy diet, doesn't junk food feel like lead in your stomach? Likewise, your old pattern may excite you when it shows up in the form of a new lover, but it's going to make you feel lousy later. A well-balanced meal probably won't satisfy your sweet tooth, and a well-balanced relationship won't satisfy your desire for drama or supply a constant endorphin or adrenaline rush. But it will be easier. It will be more satisfying over time. You can always find a new sport or hobby to give you any sought-after excitement.

The rest of this chapter will examine the most common issues that destroy relationships.

Bruce Logan

BINGING AND PURGING: COMMITMENTPHOBIA

Do your lovers seem to come and go, sometimes at a rapid pace? Do the majority of your relationships last six months or less? When you find a "can't get enough of you" passionate connection, does it end as quickly as it started? Even if the relationship lasts a year or longer, wasn't there a clear turning point after which things were never the same?

A large percentage of my clients come to me to learn how to get their boyfriend or girlfriend back after a sudden, devastating breakup. It's inconceivable to most of them how distant and cold their once incredibly loving partner is now being. It's always very clear to me when a commitmentphobe has broken a client's heart. Helping these clients understand is the only way to help them let go.

What makes commitmentphobia so hard to recognize and even comprehend at first is that most people, both men and women, who say they're looking for commitment or marriage are actually doing just that. Most of them want to be in a loving relationship with all of their heart, and many even want to get married and create a family. Most people don't experience any commitment issues until something triggers them. What causes lovers to get hurt is that the better the relationship, the more anxiety a commitmentphobe feels. This is the result of their conscious desire battling with their subconscious fear. Since they consciously know they want a good relationship, they usually assume their partner is wrong for them when they find they are just not happy in the relationship. In reality, their unhappiness is brought about because their partner is such a good choice for them that it triggers their commitmentphobia. As they start to recognize a true commitment might actually come to fruition, they become increasingly anxious and they withdraw. Sometimes by just getting space and creating distance in the relationship, but many times they suddenly bail out completely. Then the abandoned partner is devastated and usually has a very difficult time letting go.

One client, whom I'll call Kevin, came to me in utter disbelief. His girlfriend of three years, whom I'll call Tina, had been pushing him for two years to get married. She finally gave up and broke up with him. It took him less than twenty-four hours to propose. They passionately made love all night, intentionally trying to conceive a baby. In the morning, as Kevin got ready for work, Tina blissfully described her plan to move all her things into his place by the time he got home. He happily agreed and went off to work. Later that day he came home to possibly the biggest shock of his life—a good-bye note. A short one at that, it simply read, "I can't do this." Tina was gone. Kevin tried calling her, but she refused to talk and eventually changed her number.

The sad fact about that story is that it's really not at all shocking to me. Commitmentphobia is very common. I hear similar stories all the time. I've even experienced a few of my own. That's partly what drove me to become a relationship coach. This is the part that is hard for most jilted lovers to accept: it's your own passive commitment issues that cause you to choose commitmentphobes.

Kevin loved Tina very much. He considered her the love of his life. But as happy as he was with her, he couldn't bring himself to ask her to marry him. As I learned more about Tina, it became clear to me that she was emotionally unavailable. She couldn't talk about her feelings and constantly created space in the relationship. That's what allowed Kevin to openly love her. His own commitment issues caused him to choose someone who wasn't completely available to him. The only reason Tina wanted to marry him was because he didn't want to marry her. Subconsciously she was gravely afraid of commitment, so knowing Kevin wouldn't commit to her was the only reason she could openly love him. Consciously she wanted to get married and have a baby. The more she asked Kevin to give her that, the more she was subconsciously quieting her anxiety about it actually happening. As soon as he agreed to a commitment, it took her less than twenty-four hours to panic and run away.

When I suggested to Kevin that it was actually better for him that she had left so quickly, he couldn't see that. But I told him that without counseling it was inevitable that she would escape from a true commitment to anyone. When I suggested that if she had waited, she would probably have left him at the altar or after she had conceived his baby, he said, "Oh my God, you're right! That would have been much worse." Helping Kevin see all the ways that Tina was not actually a good choice for him, allowed him to begin to accept the breakup. Acknowledging his own commitment fears helped him start to recognize who might be a good choice for him.

Now, of course that story is being told from my educated perspective. From Tina's perspective, Kevin was a great guy. He possessed all the traits she wanted in a man, which is why she wanted to marry him. After two years of begging him to give her what she wanted, his lack of enthusiasm to marry her finally killed her feelings for him. She just didn't love him anymore. That was Tina's perception. Our perception is our reality; Tina was never coming back.

Kevin couldn't believe she was never coming back. He thought they had a great relationship and set out to prove to Tina how much he did indeed love her. His anxiety about being abandoned was skyrocketing. As she continued to reject him, he started to get angry. His anger accelerated her anxiety until she just shut down. She changed her phone number and moved away. All his frantic attempts to win her back just convinced her he was definitely not the one for her.

This is the cold, hard truth about being left by a commitmentphobe. She left because her anxiety was overwhelming. The only way she might possibly come back was if she got enough distance from the relationship for her anxiety to subside. Without anxiety, she would be able to feel her true feelings. If she did genuinely love Kevin, she may come back. But without counseling, her anxiety would return and she would ultimately leave again. Even if she got counseling, there is no guarantee she would then feel Kevin was a good choice for her. His unavailability was subconsciously why she had wanted him.

Most people don't recognize the underlying fear that drove their lover away. It doesn't make sense, so they drive themselves crazy trying to make sense of it. They plead their case and act out, and sometimes their own anxiety causes them to behave insecurely or even irrationally. All of this falls on deaf ears and drives their lover further and further away.

So what you need to know is that a person who has dated a lot but has never really been in love may have no idea how much anxiety she'll feel when she finally finds *the one*. If that's you, you have to remain empowered and not act insecure when things start to melt down. Of course I realize that is a lot easier said than done, especially if you have abandonment issues. (See the section titled "Food Addiction: Abandonment Issues," page 70). It helps if you know what signs to look for.

The Symptoms

Both women and men struggle with commitment issues and exhibit the same symptoms. Change the pronouns below to pertain to you. As you read over this list, look for any behavior that you may exhibit too.

1.) Moving too fast

Subconsciously he knows it won't last, so he will pull you into the relationship with no fear. He'll go above and beyond to woo you; his focus is on the pursuit and the romance. Within a very short time, he becomes completely captivated by you and makes you feel like he has never felt this way before. He's living in today and has no thought of tomorrow, so he's comfortable to love you with reckless abandon.

2.) Talking openly about commitment

If she is truly commitmentphobic, she has probably never had a good relationship. If she genuinely wants one, she will be completely enthralled with you. She'll refer to you as "we" or "us." She'll openly make plans for your life together. But as soon as she feels confident you want a commitment too, her anxiety will kick in. Your relationship will never be the same.

3.) Too understanding

He's really sensitive to a woman's needs. He voices his dislike for men who selfishly mistreat and abandon women. He seems to truly understand what you need from him. Be careful; he may know about bad behavior firsthand—he who protests too much. He's trying to feel better about himself by acknowledging he's not as bad as other men. While he's telling you he is a good guy, he is also reassuring himself.

4.) Showing vulnerability and neediness

A true commitmentphobe spends a lot of time putting her wall up, creating distance, and running away from love. But in the beginning of a relationship, she feels safe from commitment, so her true feelings and emotions can flow freely. She'll make you feel like she trusts you and needs you, because at that moment she probably does. You may feel sorry for her and want to help her. Be warned; as soon as she starts to feel comforted, her anxiety will kick in and her wall will go back up. She'll start running again.

5.) Finding faults

He may start to find fault with you. If you have ever shown your Achilles' heel—you feel a little overweight, you don't make enough money—you gave him the information he can discredit you with. Things he may have previously supported you on, he may now turn against you. Even if you didn't show him any faults, he will find something—even trivial things. To him your faults are very real. You may feel that if you could just fix all the things he doesn't like, he'd be able to marry you. But no matter how perfect you try to be, he will always find another fault so he can avoid the commitment.

6.) Trying to escape

She may find ways to escape the relationship: going out with friends, taking trips without you, engaging in activities that don't include you. She may even cheat. As she struggles with her anxiety, she'll be confused and probably want to keep you around—just not as close as you used to be. She's feeling claustrophobic now and needs a lot of space. If you don't allow her to get space, she will end up leaving you.

The Cure

As you start to recognize potential symptoms of commitmentphobia, you have to stay true to yourself. Maintain your independence, enforce healthy boundaries, and take care of your own needs. Don't allow your partner to make you insecure and start doubting yourself. Don't give her reason—real or imagined—to leave you.

1.) Slow the pace of the relationship.

It's exciting to be swept off your feet and have a whirlwind love affair. But if you feel like the relationship could have healthy-meal potential, you have to take it slow and let true feelings evolve. Don't rearrange your schedule to be available for him or his phone calls. He doesn't need to always know what you're doing. He shouldn't feel like you're at his beck and call. Only see each other two or three times a week for the first couple months. Delay having sex with him. Postpone expressing any loving feelings or revealing too much about your deep, dark inner secrets. The longer it takes to develop true intimacy, the better chance you have of staying together.

2.) Don't bring up any topics about commitment.

Moving in together, marriage, and babies are all taboo topics with a commitmentphobe. If she brings them up, be cautious about the timing. When she knows she has you is when her anxiety will start. If she starts referring to you as "us," keep your thoughts grounded. Don't start fantasizing about your future and assuming she is *the one.* What she feels today could change at any moment. Just because she says she wants to get married doesn't mean she's going to marry you. Don't engage in any discussion about furthering a commitment— beyond just exclusivity—prior to dating at least six months. After that, if commitment talk causes her to back away, let her, and move on so you can find someone capable of a true commitment.

3.) Find out about his past.

Being sensitized to and defensive about men who have hurt women may just be him masking his own previous behavior. Ask about his past relationships. Guard your own feelings and take it really slow if he has never had his heart broken, if he has never had a long-term relationship (longer than a year), or if he says all his past partners were inappropriate in one way or another. If breakups were never his fault that means he's either hiding things or can't take responsibility for his own mistakes—which means he will repeat them. He will most likely find some way to make you inappropriate for him too.

4.) Protect yourself.

You can extend the benefit of the doubt, but trust has to be earned. Don't feel like you have to solve her problems. Her showing vulnerability too quickly doesn't mean you should too. You can be sympathetic, but do not rescue her. Don't assume because she is so vulnerable about her problems that she will be sympathetic to yours. People with commitment issues are usually very selfish. Keep your boundaries strong, and put your own needs first. Keep the relationship equal, as you don't want to make her emotionally or financially dependent on you. Chapter 7, "Your Place Setting," will help you with healthy boundaries.

5.) Don't be insecure.

If he starts criticizing you or finding fault, he is being judgmental—and you should calmly tell him so. Even if you agree with him or think what he is saying is true, don't let that feed your insecurity. Don't ever lose sight of the fact that he is supposed to be your supportive partner. If he is bringing up an issue that is truly an obstacle in your relationship, then tell him you would like to work out a solution together. After you resolve it, if he finds something else to pick on, you can be assured he will never be happy with you—or anyone else. He's looking for perfection. Do not let him damage your self-esteem! It is time for you to move on and find someone truly supportive.

6.) Give your partner healthy space.

Remember, your partner is feeling anxiety. Giving her time to allow her anxiety to subside is good for both of you. Find other things to do to keep your focus off of her and to make you happy. Take a class, join a charity, or start a hobby. Spend some quality time with your friends or family, but don't talk about her. The more you maintain your independence, the happier your mate—and your relationship—will be.

Note: Women feel their feelings in the moment, but men usually have to go off on their own to feel their feelings. If you're a woman, giving your man space is good for you too.

If your partner does leave—you have to let him go. Anything you do to try to get him to stay will only push him away more. I know it's hard to just let go of someone you love, but you don't want someone who doesn't want you! Love yourself most. There is an old saying that is very relevant for commitmentphobes:

> "If you love something set it free. If it comes back to you it's yours, if not it never was."

Food for Thought

Probably most importantly, if you have had a string of failed relationships because of your partner being unavailable in one way or another (which should have been revealed to you in the pattern-identifying exercise), take a look at your own issues. People with passive commitment issues subconsciously seek out unavailable people too. Truly available people won't be attractive to you until you acknowledge your own subconscious fear. Have you become uninterested in someone who was totally into you and offering you a true commitment? Then you were taking the active commitmentphobic role. Commitment fear can switch back and forth between active and passive characteristics. I highly recommend reading

He's Scared, She's Scared[15] by Steven Carter and Julia Sokol. It describes commitmentphobic characteristics in great detail.

Having abandonment issues makes it even harder to accept that you might have commitment issues. People with abandonment issues usually want a committed relationship with all of their heart, but unfortunately they're usually attracted to people with commitment issues. If you're saying, "I didn't know he was commitmentphobic when I fell in love with him," I hear you. But what you need to hear is that subconsciously you actually did know this about him, and that is why he was attractive to you.

Do you fear your lovers leaving you? Do you have a hard time letting go when they do? Do you romanticize failed relationships to be better than they actually were? The next section will help you respond better when the anxiety of feeling abandoned overwhelms you.

Bruce Logan

FOOD ADDICTION: ABANDONMENT ISSUES

Food addicts eat when they aren't hungry. They'll continue to eat despite negative consequences, such as weight gain and poor health. As with any substance addiction, stopping the destructive behavior is extremely difficult. Similarly, love addicts have an insatiable appetite for love. When they feel attracted to a person, they immediately idealize that person into the perfect partner, becoming blind to reality. They fall in love too easily,

---

[15] Steven Carter and Julia Sokol, *He's Scared, She's Scared: Understanding the Hidden Fears that Sabotage Your Relationships* (New York: Delacorte Press, 1995).

even if their love is not returned. They may settle for a relationship that is less than they deserve, become needy, and tolerate extreme dysfunction or abuse. They may fantasize constantly and change who they are to suit their partner. When their relationships end, love addicts experience extreme withdrawal. They have a hard time letting go and often chase after the person who has rejected them.

Love addiction develops when someone is neglected in early childhood. Whether a parent leaves, dies, or is distracted by other things (such as alcohol, drugs, or a career), the child doesn't attach to the mother. A child who is frequently left alone doesn't learn how to connect and interact with other people. A lonely little girl usually creates elaborate fantasies of being rescued by her version of prince charming. These fantasies trigger chemical reactions in her brain that literally make her feel warm and comforted. These powerful fantasies created by the child make up for her feelings of aloneness and neglect. She gets addicted to that feeling, and it's mistaken for feelings of love.[16]

When that neglected child grows up, she starts projecting her fantasy lover onto any boy who will pay attention to her. When it doesn't work out, she is terrified and will do anything not to be alone. Love addiction comes in many different forms, and the symptoms vary. It's more common in women, but men can develop it too. It mirrors many of the symptoms of codependence.

Fear of abandonment usually accompanies love addiction. Most people fear abandonment on some level, whether they recognize it or not. Like love addiction, the fear of abandonment also comes from our childhood experiences. It develops not only as a result of obvious abandonment, such as a parent leaving or dying, but also from growing up with an emotionally withdrawn parent or a loved one who threatens to leave, lies, or does not keep promises. It is even thought to potentially develop in infancy if an infant's needs are not met. The reason fear of abandonment is so common is that it can form in many different and subtle ways. The symptoms can range from mild to debilitating. People

---

[16] Mellody, Pia; Andrea Wells Miller; and Keith Miller. *Facing Love Addiction: Giving Yourself the Power to Change the Way You Love: The Love Connection to Codependence.* New York, NY: HarperCollins, 1992.

usually don't experience abandonment fear until something triggers it as an adult—typically a romantic relationship.

You may have never stopped to label it fear of abandonment, but if you have it, you probably recognize some of the symptoms. Are you uncomfortable being alone? Do you need your partner's constant attention? Do you fear him cheating or leaving you? Do you have a hard time trusting? Do you need constant contact with your partner when he is not around?

Symptoms of Abandonment Issues

- **Reaching Out**

  You habitually reach out to the person you're in a relationship with. You become needy for communication and usually end up doing what you fear most—pushing your lover away.

- **Need for Constant Reassurance**

  You need repeated reassurance that you are loved or desired. You may frequently ask, "Do you love me?" Or you may want constant attention and affection.

- **Panic Attacks**

  Your reaction is disproportionate to reality. You feel anxiety if your lover is late, doesn't answer your call, or is unavailable in any way.

- **Emotional Blackmail**

  You have threatened to harm yourself in any way as an ultimatum to get what you want. Trying or threatening to kill yourself if your partner leaves you is a desperate act when fearing abandonment.

- **Leaving Relationships**

  You have so much fear of being left or rejected that you leave first so you can control it. You may go from relationship to relationship, never staying long enough to get hurt.

- **Complacent Behavior**

  You'll go along to get along. You'll do whatever your partner wants, regardless of you how you feel, just to keep him or her with you.

- **Lowered Sense of Self-Worth**

    You identify yourself through your relationship. You feel like you're nothing if you're not in a relationship.

Sometimes abandonment issues are not that clear. Maybe you always have a relationship and bounce from one to the next without hesitation, never allowing yourself to be alone. Possibly you had a relationship in which everything seemed fine until your partner pulled away or left; then you suddenly became needy and felt insecure. You may have experienced anxiety or panic attacks even though you had never experienced them in the past.

I had a client, whom I'll call Jack, who came to me in a panic because his girlfriend, whom I'll call Teresa, broke up with him. He was having extreme separation anxiety, but he was also in disbelief because he had never felt that way before. He didn't know how to deal with it. To further confuse his situation, he made it clear to me as he described the relationship that *he* was the one who hadn't wanted the relationship. In fact, he had active commitment issues. Jack fell head over heels for Teresa, but as they were condo shopping, he started to escape the relationship. Teresa realized that Jack wasn't taking her phone calls as readily as he had used to, she started to become insecure. He started to stay away on business more frequently, so Teresa asked him if he still wanted to move in with her. His hesitation when he answered, even though he said yes, triggered her very sensitive abandonment issues. She started to pull away.

When Teresa pulled away, Jack's commitment anxiety quieted down, so he continued the relationship. But Teresa became a different person. She was incredibly selfish, rude, and even mean to Jack's family. She cheated on him openly and was unapologetic. When Jack found out about the cheating, he didn't break up with her, and he didn't even really get angry; he just chose to stop having sex with her. The relationship was junk-food. She'd behave incredibly badly, and he would escape but still romanticize the relationship. Finally, Jack made a career decision that would make him more available to her. Teresa panicked and broke up with him. Jack fell apart with anxiety from the abandonment.

That's when he came to me to find out how to get her back. As he described all the truly horrible and selfish things Teresa had done, he laughed and acknowledged he knew he didn't want to marry her. Even after he had clearly articulated why this girl was not a good choice for him, he would continually break down and ask, "So how do I get her back?" Jack had become addicted to her. He was emotionally idealizing her to be the perfect partner. He had never before felt the kind of love that he had initially felt for Teresa. Just like a heroin junkie, he was longing for and chasing that original high. Jack spent hundreds of hours on the phone with me, his siblings, his friends, his mother, and anyone else who would listen to him agonize about Teresa. Everyone he spoke with repeatedly pointed out how wrong Teresa was for him. Intellectually, he could agree; he knew he did not want her—he didn't even want to have sex with her. But his extreme anxiety over feeling abandoned kept him longing for her. His addiction needed a fix; he just wanted her to call.

I'm sharing this story because it has the elements of love addiction, commitmentphobia, and fear of abandonment. Very commonly these three issues can be found together, and they frequently switch between people in a relationship. For example, Jack started out with active commitment issues. When Teresa pulled back, she relieved him of a deeper commitment and he started to become addicted to her. He spent a lot of money and did some really nice things for Teresa, all while she was behaving badly. When she left him, he felt abandoned. Feeling abandoned actually comforted his commitment issues, because as long as he was pining for Teresa, he would never achieve a real commitment. But that was all subconscious; consciously, Jack was suffering. Teresa, on the other hand, had very deep abandonment issues. Her father had left just after she was born. Her family never heard from him again, and her mother shut down emotionally. Her father physically abandoned her, and her mother emotionally abandoned her. She could only feel safe in the relationship while Jack was 100 percent there and committed to her. As soon as she no longer felt safe, she needed to abandon him before he could abandon her. She needed to control it. Teresa also struggled with commitment issues. She couldn't trust anyone to stay and give her a real commitment, so she always pushed lovers away.

Entire books have been dedicated to the individual characteristics of love addiction, codependence, fear of abandonment, and commitmentphobia. You'll find some great ones in this book's reference list. They are complicated issues. I can't possibly identify all of the origins and manifestations of each disorder and explain how to heal them in this chapter. However, behavioral modification can be very effective. You can learn how to respond better when you feel anxiety, panic, or fear. You can monitor and control behavior situationally so that you don't sabotage and destroy your relationships. You can use your thoughts very proactively to change even your brain. This chapter is intended to give you some tools to help you better manage your anxiety.

Hunger Pains

Human beings are creatures of habit. Addicts are beings of extreme habit. When two people break up, what they initially have to deal with is breaking the habit of interacting with each other. It's a habit to call to share things that happen, it's a habit to have an automatic date on weekends, and it's a habit to let your thoughts focus on what the other person in a relationship is doing. The best way to break a habit is to replace it with something else. That's why many people go right into another relationship. (See "Between-Meal Snacks," page 129). The healthy thing to do is shift all that loving energy toward you. Create a new habit of taking care of you. Start by taking care of what you think.

In the above story, Jack was clinging to the fantasy of who Teresa was to him in the beginning. What he needed to do was acknowledge who Teresa truly is. Love addicts, codependents, and people who fear abandonment all have an extremely difficult time letting go when a relationship ends. They cling to the hope of what the relationship could have been. They cherish the amazing connection they once had together. But that reality no longer exists.

Hope is a powerful thing. But when your hope is based on a fantasy that isn't real, hope will only keep you in pain. While you remain addicted to a food that isn't available to you, your hunger will never go away. However, when the person you're hungering for is junk-food, that is a real gift to help you let go. Breaking up is never easy. But when you can truly acknowledge that a person is not good for you—and never will be—your hunger pain will turn into a healthy appetite again.

First and foremost, you have to stop thinking about your ex-partner. Every time you allow your thoughts to run the highlight reel—memories of all the good times you had together—your brain responds as if it is happening all over again. That's why you do it. Reexperiencing loving memories gives you the fix you're craving. Then, when you stop, you're snapped back to reality. The pain and withdrawal are just as intense as when the breakup initially happened. You're back to day one of trying to let go. For love addicts and many others, the pain of facing that reality over and over is more than they can bear. So they retreat into the comfort of their thoughts whenever possible and talk about their love to whoever will listen. Have you ever met someone who is still committed to a relationship that ended years before? And who refuses to date anyone else because their soul mate was the one true love of their life—even if their love passed away or is with someone else? People such as these are comforted by their thoughts. They develop intense fantasies combined with their idealized memories to give them the relationship they crave. It's enough for them because your brain doesn't distinguish between thinking and doing. So if you're going through a breakup, ask yourself if just the memory of a relationship is enough for you. If not, you have to stop thinking good thoughts about the relationship so you can move on.

In recent decades, neuroscientists have discovered neuroplasticity— the brain's ability to change its structure and function in response to experience. More recently they added the power of the mind to change the brain. [17] What that means is that you can use your thoughts to create new functions in your brain. That's what makes visualization and meditation so effective. It's also the basis for cognitive behavioral therapy (CBT), which involves using repetitive thought processes to think your way out of depression and anxiety. So if you use your thoughts positively, you can help yourself feel better. On the other hand, if you use your thoughts negatively, you can make yourself depressed, fearful, and addicted to a lover who doesn't want you. Fantasies are the equivalent of visualization. Running the mental highlight reel of all the good times of a relationship after you are no longer together gives your brain mixed messages. This causes you to create your own confusion—and heartache. After a breakup, you should only allow yourself to think about the negatives.

---

[17] Sharon Begley, "The Brain: How The Brain Rewires Itself," *Time*, Dec. 3, 2012, http://www.time.com/time/magazine/article/0,9171,1580438,00.html.

Write a cons list. Forget the pros; they are irrelevant to you now. Handwrite your list, your brain processes information better when your hand physically creates words on the page.

- Handwrite on a piece of paper all the junk-food ingredients your ex and the relationship had.

- Write your list and then read it back several times.

- Memorize it.

- When you catch yourself thinking positively about your ex-partner, switch your thinking to something negative.

- Make it a habit.

It may be hard at first, but with a little practice, you'll soon be wondering why you ever wanted that junk-food in the first place.

Cooking with Gas vs. Electric

Your perception is your reality. Your brain receives stimuli and information and forms an opinion. What makes relationships tricky is that no two brains perceive information the same way, not even in identical twins. So what seems very real to you may seem ridiculous to someone else. This doesn't make either of you wrong; it just means that your perceptions are different. When a meal breaks up with you, he or she does so because his or her perception is that you don't work together. If you perceive it differently, you find yourself tempted to try to change his or her perception. But you can never control someone else. You can only control you, so it's *your* perception you need to change.

We do have free will over our perceptions. We can choose to seek additional information and consider other people's perceptions as a way to fine-tune our own perceptions. We can also choose to adopt a positive perception that will give us power.

How do you deal with rejection? Change your perception. Stop viewing it as rejection. If some clueless meal doesn't see how truly special you are, then you don't want her anyway! It doesn't matter how great you may think she is. Think again. If she doesn't appreciate you, then she's not good enough for you. Period. Let her go, and move on to the next. I do know that can be a difficult pill to swallow, especially when you really like somebody. But if you start jumping through hoops and doing other silly things, trying to make her want you, then you're negatively changing her perception. You're making yourself less attractive, and you're damaging your self-esteem. Love yourself first. Don't waste any precious time on any person who doesn't adore you. It's all a matter of how you choose to perceive it. Focus on her negative attributes and trust that there will be someone better. If you don't want someone, then you can't be rejected.

There will be more information about using your thoughts to help you feel better in chapter 7, "Relationship Crash Diet."

Learning to Fast

Fasting is the act of willingly abstaining from consuming any food or drink for a certain period of time. The purpose of fasting is to make one healthier. A great tool you can learn to apply when you feel the anxiety of abandonment is to just do nothing. Fast. Tell yourself to push the pause button, and don't respond or react to anything. Instead, take some long, deep breaths and let them out slowly. Breathing deeply is a CBT technique that helps calm anxiety. It is physiologically impossible to feel anxiety while you are breathing deeply. Try it.

The next time you're feeling anxious or starting to panic because you haven't heard from your meal, or because he rejected you, yelled at you, or sent a text or e-mail that upset you, pause and breathe deeply. When your mind starts racing with wild thoughts of retaliation, rebuttal, or revenge, stop and breathe deeply. Say to yourself, "Push the pause button." Whenever I have a client relating his fear—his "what ifs" and assumptions—I always tell him to push the pause button. I frequently tell myself that too; it works, and that's why I'm passing it on to you. It won't solve all your problems, and it won't prevent future panic attacks, but it will get you through this moment and today and prevent any relationship damage. Keeping your thoughts in the present is another great tool for calming anxiety. Don't think about anything that you can't do *for yourself* right now, in the moment. Your thoughts control and create your feelings. Keep your thoughts off of what is causing your anxiety.

Clients have said, "When I hear bad news, I feel as though I have been punched in the stomach. I didn't think that up; it's a physical reaction." But that's actually an emotional response. Your feelings are separate from your emotions. The emotional center in your brain is the quickest to respond in any situation. It takes the reasoning part of your brain a little longer to engage. But as soon as it does, you have free will to choose how you want to respond. Your thoughts are in control. That's why you should take a few breaths before responding to a stimulus; not just so you can calm down, but also so a logical part of your brain has time to weigh in so you can respond intelligently instead of emotionally.

If you accept that your thoughts truly are in control, you can use them to comfort your emotions. You can consciously think to take deep breaths to calm your anxiety. You can think about the positive things. There is always a positive side; find it. You can create a pleasant, happy fantasy in your mind (that doesn't include your love interest) and escape to that tranquil place whenever you feel upset or angry. So when you do get that punched-in-the-stomach feeling, your thoughts can make it go away. Or they can prolong it and make it worse. Which choice sounds better to you?

Fast Delivery

Electronic communication has changed relationships—and not for the better. For people with abandonment issues, and especially for those who struggle with anxiety, the ability to immediately communicate your feelings is a bad thing. Good communication is the foundation of a happy relationship. But bombarding your meal with every emotional thought that runs through your head can be disastrous. Too many very smart people succumb to the self-defeating act of texting or e-mailing their lover in a moment of emotional insecurity, frequently when they are tipsy or drunk, forgoing any rational judgment. The lure to instantly deliver your deepest feelings—positive or negative—may feel satisfying in the moment, but the consequences of pressing the send button are rarely beneficial.

Just because you have the ability to do something doesn't mean you should do it. Just because you can send a message immediately doesn't mean you deserve an immediate response. I can't even tell you how many clients have called me upset and all worked up about a text message. In the middle of the day I frequently hear, "I sent him a text three hours ago and he hasn't replied." To which I always say, "What does he do for a living? Maybe he's working and will reply later." He usually does—when it's convenient for him.

One client called because the guy she really liked took her to dinner for her birthday. It was their third date. The next day she sent him a text that said, "Thank you for my birthday dinner ☺ it was great to see you!" He texted, "My pleasure. I enjoyed our time together. Once again Happy Bday. May this year be your best year yet. ☺" She was upset because she thought she was never going to see him again. She interpreted him telling her to have a great year to mean she would not see him in that year. What would you think? It sounds to me like it went well. Saying "Have a great year" is just like wishing someone a happy new year. She was just feeling insecure.

Another client sent a text to the guy she was casually sleeping with that said something like, "You marked your territory with a love bite on my neck last night; no other guy is going to want to be with me." He responded, "Good." She was upset that he thought it was good he left a mark on her. I shared that I thought he meant it was good she wouldn't be with any other men. She liked that interpretation better. Still another client complained that whenever she texted her guy, "I miss you," he only ever replied with a smiley face. She thought that meant he didn't miss her and that he just liked that she missed him. On talking to her further, she revealed that he only ever responded with a smiley face to anything. But when she texted her feelings, the generic response sparked her insecurity.

The problem with any written communication is that its context can be misconstrued. Without the inflection of voice to help interpret its meaning, you may take what is written the wrong way. So may the receiver of your written communications. One's perception is one's reality. Your relationship is too important to leave up to chance. A text may instigate some horrible miscommunication that damages or even ends the relationship, usually because someone acted on a fleeting emotional impulse.

Emotional hijackings such as these completely give away your power and rarely produce positive results. People do not respond well to dramatic information thrown at them randomly. Would you? If you're feeling insecure or upset about something while you're not in your meal's company, you have to be patient. Push the pause button! Writing out your feelings is an excellent way to process them; just *do not* send them! Writing it down will get it off your chest and allow you to stop obsessing. Review what you wrote the next day when you can have a fresh perspective. If you still feel like you need to share your thoughts, ask to schedule a time to talk face-to-face.

However, if your partner has told you it's over and you feel you're never going to see him again, then he definitely doesn't need to know how you feel. Maintain your power. If you pour your heart out to him in an e-mail, you'll just squash any positive feelings he may still have. Both men and women have told me that they think jilted lovers are crazy when they send e-mails pleading their case about why the relationship works when they have been told it doesn't. You have to respect a meal's boundaries. If you genuinely think you might be able to work it out, then you need to do that face-to-face, or at the very least on the phone. It needs to be a two-way conversation so you can be sure your feelings are acknowledged. E-mails will leave you vulnerable because no response is required. If your meal is not willing to talk about it further, then he or she is not worth any more of your precious time. The section "Force-Feeding" on page 85 will help you with letting go.

Just to be clear, until you're in a committed relationship, sending warm and fuzzy texts can be detrimental to your connection. They may feel needy or smothering to your potential meal. As a woman, you can fall in love and can process your feelings while you're in the company of your guy. If you are a right-handed man, you need to step back and take a break from your woman to process your feelings. Women's brains and left-handed men's brains can think and feel at the same time.[18] Right-handed men can only do one at a time. So give your right-handed man that space to step back from thinking and switch to feeling. Don't invade his space with text messages. If you're a right-handed man, try to extend

---

[18]Dr. Patricia Allen and Sandra Harmon, *Getting to "I Do": The Secret to Doing Relationships Right!* (New York: Quill, 2002).

some empathy if your woman sends emotional texts that you think are illogical; given a little time, it may feel right.

For women, let the man be the man. Making first contact is exhibiting masculine energy. If you like men with masculine energy, your male energy will repel them like the negative charge of a magnet. If you initiate the contact, it's much easier for a man to simply reply, but that doesn't mean he really *wanted* to see you. People do what they want to do. If he wants to contact you, he will. Give him the time to do so. If you initiate the contact, you will never know if he really likes you or if you just made it easy for him and he thought, "Why not?" Maybe he was just being polite. In all of my above examples regarding text messaging, my female clients had initiated the contact—and then they felt insecure at the response. If you would not call a man, do not text or e-mail him. Push the pause button! Too many women today are giving away their power by texting men. Men are noticing and getting lazy; they're letting the women do all the work, but that's screwing up the natural selection process. If he likes you and you don't text him, you'll stand out from other women in a good way. It will make him want you more. Anything worth having is worth working for. Allow him to work for you. He's not the right one for you if he doesn't.

Electronic communication is impersonal and doesn't belong in a personal relationship. It's really easy to forget there is a real human being with real feelings on the other end of your device. So give yourself some guidelines to live by.

E-mail and Text Recipes

- Never e-mail or text when you're impaired: angry, sad, or otherwise emotional, or under the influence of any substance.

- Never e-mail or text when you've just ended an emotional phone conversation. Let sleeping dogs lie.

- If you wouldn't deliver your message in person, then don't send it via text or e-mail. Remember, the receiver has feelings, too (even if he or she is not good at showing them).

- Don't use text or e-mail as a replacement for phone calls. One-on-one communication is best. Don't schedule all your dates through texts.

- Don't hide behind e-mails. It's really easy to type out what you want and just hit send. But that won't get you the kind of response you need, and it gives your meal permission to do the same. Don't be surprised if he or she breaks up with you through e-mail. Anything that will potentially alter your relationship needs to be done in person or at least speaking on the phone.

- Only send a text or e-mail if it will positively benefit your relationship and it cannot be misconstrued, such as messages stating that you're running late or communicating other logistical information.

- The man should be the pursuer. Ladies, don't send texts to initiate contact.

Weight Retention

People with abandonment issues can need constant reassurance that they are wanted and loved. They have only short-term memory when it comes to their lover's positive feelings or intentions. A female client recently called me upset with the man she is dating. He travels a lot for business. He had texted her from another city to say hi and to tell her he'd be back to New York soon and was looking forward to a big hug. But he didn't say anything about how he feels about her. She was angry that he was so unexpressive, and she was going to tell him she didn't want to see him again. But thankfully she wanted to run it by me first. You see, they have only been dating a short while and have been having a hard time coordinating their schedules. But the last time he was in the city, he sent some very intimate texts. He told her he thinks about her constantly and thinks she is amazing. That prompted a very intense conversation about their feelings and intentions. She really likes him and was happy he was being so communicative. He was going to be traveling nonstop for a few weeks, but he promised he'd set aside quality time to spend with her when he got back. She agreed to give him a chance. However, he's not very communicative when he travels, so she got insecure. She feared he had changed his mind, and she needed reassurance of his feelings. Her fear of being abandoned was causing her to want to abandon him first. What she truly wanted was for him to love her. She was about to sabotage that opportunity.

In my opinion, he had established that he cared. He prepared her for his absence by letting her know that he would be unavailable until he got back. The very fact that he texted her to touch base was reassurance the plan was still on. She was just feeling needy and wanted to hear his feelings again. Most men (and some women) aren't that expressive. They usually say what they mean and then feel like it's established. If she had changed her mind about seeing him, I think he would have been confused as to why. Nothing had changed on his side.

I suggested she wait to see how he treated her when he got back. Then if it wasn't enough for her, she could renegotiate the relationship. She had told him she'd give him a chance, so I thought she at least needed to do that. She agreed. She then felt bad she had been standoffish to his text. It was good she had me to reassure her. That's why I'm sharing this story with you. You need to learn to reassure yourself if you're feeling abandoned. Push the pause button. Don't create drama where there isn't any.

When I recommend keeping your thoughts in the present, that doesn't mean that you forget everything you knew up until this point. You have to retain any loving communication you receive until there is new evidence that something changed—solid evidence attained face-to-face. If you catch yourself feeling insecure and doubting his feelings or the relationship—push the pause button. Then rewind a little and examine what you already know. Take your imagination out of it, and don't decide for him what he is feeling. Review chapter 1, "The Recipe and Food Envy," page 45, and wait for your meal to make the next move.

Constant Cravings

One of the primary and most common characteristics of love addiction is the overwhelming fear of being alone. You don't feel whole if you're not in a relationship. You can't enjoy your own company. The fear of never finding someone to love you can be so powerful it causes you to act needy and even desperate. It's that fear that is actually preventing true love from coming to you. Energy is contagious. When you yearn for something too much, you create "must-have" energy that only pushes it away. A great analogy to illustrate what I'm saying is being in the ocean, out past the surf where the water is over your head. Imagine a beach ball floating several feet away. If you start swimming toward it, you'll create wake in the water that will push it farther away from you—farther out to sea. But if you stay still, the ball will have an opportunity to float toward you on its own. The wind or the surf may push it toward you. Of course there is a chance it won't come to you. But if you try to force it, it definitely won't come to you.

You can't force someone to love you. The more you try to manipulate someone, the more you push them away. I know it's very scary not to be able to control things—especially when they affect your safety. A love addict doesn't feel safe when he or she doesn't have a partner. But you need to stop being your own worst enemy. Push the pause button and take care of you. You will be much more attractive if you maintain your power and act nutritiously. You can read more about maintaining your power in chapter 7, "Relationship Crash Diet."

Force-Feeding

Force-feeding is the act of feeding a person or animal against its will. People with eating disorders will sometimes refuse to eat because of an extreme fear of gaining weight. When hospitalized, they can be force-fed by a tube to give them life-sustaining nutrients, but that doesn't help them emotionally or make them *want* to eat.

If you are still contacting an ex-lover who has told you she doesn't want to be with you anymore, you are attempting to force-feed her. She has made up her mind, and *nothing* you can do can change that. Any attempt at connection or communication *will* make things worse for you. She may be polite at first and try to listen to what you have to say. That doesn't mean she wants you again; she doesn't. Trying harder will only propel your anxiety—it will not get you what you want. Put yourself in her shoes.

I have a girlfriend, whom I'll call Mary, who found out the man she had been dating for about six months was married. She broke up with him. They initially talked to try to gain some closure, but he didn't want closure. He wanted to keep seeing her. He had been telling her all sorts of lies, and she was confused. She had thought she loved him, but she had no idea who he even was. She just wanted to be done with him. She kept telling him it was over and that she didn't want to talk to him anymore. He wasn't hearing her. He relentlessly tried to change her mind. He kept calling nonstop at all hours of the day and night. He even showed up at her apartment unannounced. Thankfully, Mary has a doorman who kept him out.

Mary had introduced Danny to me, and we all had been working on a possible business idea together. I have to admit, I was shocked to hear he was married too. When we first met, he said he was divorced. Mary had been talking to me about his obsessive communication attempts, and I had encouraged her not to take his calls anymore. Then he started filling up her voicemail. I suggested she delete the messages without listening to them to avoid any further negative stimulation. She told him over and over to please just leave her alone. He wouldn't. Finally, Mary asked me if I would call Danny and ask him to stop contacting her. Since we had been working together, he had previously called me to say he was backing out of the project, before I knew what had happened. I thought he might take my call as an excuse to find out about Mary. Luckily, I got his voicemail and left a firm message saying, "Danny, you have to stop harassing Mary."

I actually got a nice call back from Danny. He was mortified that I had called his communication attempts harassment. But it gave him an epiphany. He suddenly realized that what he was doing wasn't effective. Quite to the contrary, it was harmful. He finally stopped. The good news for Mary was that the experience helped her get over him. He was far from the man she thought he was. I'm sharing this story with you in case you are doing what Danny was doing to Mary.

I fully understand what it's like to feel abandoned by someone you love with all of your heart. I also understand the separation anxiety that drives you to reach out to your love to try to change his or her mind. I even understand what's it's like to be confused and to be desperately searching to figure out what happened. Any new information you discover you want to share with the object of your desire—to help him understand too—to change his mind. But none of that works. You have to accept his boundary that it is over. That is his reality. You are only making yourself look needy and unattractive. If your ex-partner has his own anxiety, all your anxiety is making his much worse.

I had a client named Jenny who had been in a two-year relationship with a man named Brian. There were a lot of really good things about their relationship. There were also some deal-breaking qualities that didn't work for Jenny. She had done a lot of self-growth work, and she wanted Brian to mature along with her. She regularly talked to him about her feelings and desires. He could always acknowledge his issues, and he would promise to make changes. However, he never actually accomplished any modifications. He had gotten comfortable in knowing that she was his, and he was lazy about being a good partner. He even started to become passive aggressive with her, belittling things she liked or wanted to do. On some level, he knew he was wrong; he started to make Jenny wrong so he could feel better about himself. Jenny finally got fed up. She got tired of hearing empty words, so she decided it was time to leave the relationship.

Brian had a meltdown. He began pouring his heart out to her in every way her could—e-mails, texts, and voicemail. She took his calls for a while to try to help him gain closure. That's not what Brian wanted. He wanted Jenny back. He began trying very hard to make positive changes for himself, but it was just too late. He had had his chance; he hadn't stepped up and done any work to remain a good partner for her. She had tried everything she could. Now she was done.

One night, Jenny was home alone and her dog started barking like crazy at the window. She went to look and saw a man in the bushes. She screamed. As the man started to run away, she recognized that it was Brian. He had been watching her. That's how desperate he had gotten; he just wanted to see her. He needed to see if she was with anyone else. She wasn't. Brian couldn't understand why she didn't want him anymore. He figured it must be because she met someone new. He couldn't understand why she wouldn't give him another chance. But Jenny had given him many chances. He just never took her seriously. He never thought she'd leave.

This story is another example of why you have to believe people when they tell you things about themselves. (See "Read the Ingredients" on page 41). It is also an example of how a normal person can become a stalker. Brian was stalking Jenny. I'm sure he didn't consider it stalking; he was just giving in to his abandonment anxiety. However, that kind of behavior is considered stalking. Both of these stories were about men, but women frequently behave the same way. When a person has told you he or she doesn't want contact from you, violating his or her wishes with *any* form of contact becomes harassment and/or stalking. You most definitely do not want a restraining order filed against you.

My older cousin taught me a valuable lesson about other people's feelings when I was just six years old. Maybe this analogy can help you too. I had wanted a cat with all of my heart and soul, and my favorite aunt had finally gotten me one. I was so happy to have that cat that I couldn't put her down. No matter how much she struggled and meowed to be let go, I just wanted to cuddle her more. If she did get away, I'd chase her all over the house until I caught her again. I simply couldn't love her enough. Then one day I was walking through the living room at my aunt's house when my cousin grabbed me and held me tight on his lap. "Let me go," I yelled. "No," he said. I started to struggle and fight, but he was much bigger than me and I couldn't get away. I started to cry, but he still wouldn't let me go. I was angry and kicking and screaming. It made no difference; he wouldn't let me go. After what seemed like an eternity, he finally released me. He asked, "Did you like that?" "No!" I said, still pouting. "That's what you do to the cat!" he said. Wow, that was awful. I got it. After that, every time she wanted to get down, I let her— even though I didn't like it.

When you love someone, it's not just about what you want. True love means wanting the other person to be happy too. It's a hard pill to swallow when what he wants is to be away from you. But the loving thing to do is to let him have what he wants. You can't force someone to love you. If you try, he may end up hating you. He almost certainly will cut you off forever. Don't give away your power. (See chapter 7: "Relationship Crash Diet").

If someone is trying to force-feed you,

- tell them firmly you want them to stop contacting you;

- stop acknowledging any of their communication;

- if they continue contact, make a written record of each attempt to reach you;

- tell friends and family—you may need emotional and physical support;

- if necessary, ask someone else to urge them to stop contacting you; and

- as a last resort only, get a restraining order. However, this may make things worse.

If you have been identifying with many of the behaviors of a love addict visit the Love Addicts Anonymous website and take their forty-question quiz to help determine if you are a love addict. They have many more helpful resources and free meetings if you think you need help.

http://www.loveaddicts.org/40questions.html

Checklist for Relieving Food Addiction

✓ Push the pause button. Breathe deeply.

✓ Keep your thoughts in the present.

✓ Find a positive perception.

✓ Don't initiate texts or e-mails. Never communicate emotions electronically.

✓ Don't create "must have" toward a person; you will only push him or her away.

✓ Respect the boundaries and wishes of any person who has broken up with you. Honor what he or she wants, not only what you want.

You don't have to be a love addict to make the wrong choices in romantic partners. But if you do tend toward being a love addict, it's even more important to be careful about whom you allow yourself to become passionately involved with. It truly is better to be by yourself than with the wrong person. While you are with Mr. or Ms. Wrong, you will never find the Mr. or Ms. Right you so desperately crave.

Quiz: Who Is Your Healthy Meal?

There is no high or low score, or even right or wrong score, for this quiz. Who your healthy meal is depends on who you are, what your needs and desires are, and what turns you on. In order to be able to find (and recognize) your healthy meal, you have to know exactly what qualities that person will possess. This quiz was designed to help you decide what is best for you in a partner.

1. What I'm most attracted to in meals is

    A.) how hot they are.

    B.) their intellect and demeanor.

    C.) what they do for a living and/or how much money they make.

2. Physically I'm most attracted to meals who are

    A.) sexy; I don't really have a specific type.

    B.) in great shape or another specific body type.

    C.) tall or short, or other specific physicality.

3. I'd never date a meal who is

    A.) shorter than I am.

    B.) making less than $100,000 a year.

    C.) more than five years older or younger than I am.

4. My idea of a romantic is

    A.) someone who showers me with gifts and attention.

    B.) someone who enjoys alone time with me (with no TV or cell phone).

    C.) someone who remembers all the details about me and the things we do together.

5. My deal-breakers are

    A.) very specific; I know exactly what junk-food flags to look for.

    B.) varied; it depends on the person.

    C.) unknown; I'm not really sure what behaviors are deal-breakers.

6. When it comes to money, I want a meal who

    A.) is frugal and saves for the future.

    B.) is generous and knows how to spend money.

    C.) has a clear budget and enjoys life while sticking to it.

7. Everyone seems to want a meal with a sense of humor. What do you consider funny?

    A.) sarcastic wit

    B.) dry, situational humor

    C.) self-deprecating observation

8. My idea of a great sex life means

    A.) frequently trying different potions and locations.

    B.) doing kinky and/or unusual things.

    C.) a great connection and spontaneity.

9. My healthy meal will have these qualities (circle all that apply):

(Note: Don't try to adapt your selections to someone you already have feelings for.)

positive	athletic	self-confident
good with children	college educated	lets me be me
financially secure	animal lover	sports fan
enjoys cooking	sensitive	cultured
compassionate	neat/tidy	family oriented

well-read	passionate	romantic
spontaneous	makes me laugh	likes to travel
affectionate	supportive	adventurous
direct	social	playful
nurturing	faithful	honest
sexual	forgiving	homebody
wants to get married	wants children	generous
accepting of my children	creative/artistic	handy
good at listening	respectful	trustworthy
a cuddler	religious	music lover

Add your own:

_____

_____

_____

10. My healthy meal won't have these qualities (circle all that apply):

(Note: Include negative experiences from past relationships and the junk-food flags from your pattern exercise on page 60.)

controlling	jealous	drinks heavily	needy
manipulative	competitive	judgmental	critical
allergic to cats	conformist	angry	political
bad-tempered	cheap	married	religious
has children	abusive	violent	an addict
unemployed	aggressive	negative	a loner
complainer	a hater	disrespectful	a player
moody	mama's boy	uses drugs	unfaithful

lazy   blamer   emotionally closed   mooch

Add your own:

_____

_____

_____

What Your Answers Should Tell You

For question 1:	For question 2:
A = 2 points	A = 6 points
B = 6 points	B = 2 points
C = 4 points	C = 4 points

For question 3:

If none of the available answers appropriately applied to you, then give yourself 6 points. If you comfortably selected one of the choices, then give yourself the designated points below.

A = 0 points

B = 2 points

C = 4 points

For question 4:	For question 5:
A = 4 points	A = 6 points
B = 2 points	B = 4 points
C = 6 points	C = 2 points

Your Total Score for Questions 1–5 _____

If you scored 8–14, your choice in meals is too vague. You're selecting your partners purely by attraction without a specific list of deal-breakers. A sign of love addiction is being more focused on initial attraction and less focused on taking the time to truly fall in love. It's great to keep an open mind, but dating by chemistry alone will only leave you open to failed and even painful relationships. Questions 9 and 10 will help you decide exactly what you need to look for in future meals.

If you scored 16–22, your choice in meals is too superficial. You're putting too much emphasis on outward appearance and material things. You need to identify the specific things you're looking for in a meal. What's most important in making a relationship work is taking care of yourself and having common values, wants, and needs. If you give someone different a chance, you might be very pleasantly surprised with what you find.

If you scored 24–30, you're on the right track. You're open to different physical types and you're looking a little deeper for more important traits. The more specific you can be, the better your chance of making a great choice. Of course that doesn't mean you should be unrealistically picky; that will just keep you alone. Questions 9 and 10 will help you decide exactly what you need to look for in future meals.

For Questions 6, 7 and 8, there are no point values. These questions are to get you thinking about what specifically is a match for you. Write your answer in your journal or on the deal-breakers list you make from questions 9 and 10.

Question 6: Money problems are the number-one cause of divorce. Most couples don't discuss how they handle money before they fall in love. Everyone has a specific blueprint for how he or she deals with money. It comes from childhood and your parents' relationship with money. In order for a couple to have a well-balanced partnership, both parties' money styles must be compatible. Make sure you discuss how you will handle money with your partner before making a true commitment.

Question 7: Laughter is great for a relationship and for your health. The couple that laughs together stays together. Just be cautious that you are never the brunt of the jokes. What can seem funny in the beginning can end up as painful. If he or she is directly making fun of you or anyone else, other than himself or herself, it's passive-aggressive hostility—and a huge junk-food flag.

Question 8: Great sex can be the foundation that keeps a relationship healthy. However, when it works, it should only be 10 percent of the relationship. Communication, commonality, and love are the most important elements. When sex doesn't work, it becomes 90 percent of the relationship. The next chapter, "Comfort Food Overindulgence," will tell you more about sex that doesn't work.

Questions 9 and 10: Go back over each quality that you circled or added and decide if it is an absolute necessity—something you can't live without or can't live with. If it is necessary to you, then write R for "requirement" next to it. If it's a quality you think would be nice but you'd be okay if you didn't get it, then write P for "preference" next to it.

You now have a deal-breaker list. Write all your requirements in your journal. Anyone you consider dating has to match your requirements. They are nonnegotiable. Don't alter them to suit a hot-looking meal.

Your preferences can be negotiable. Try not to turn down anyone because of a preference. You could be turning away a great match, and you might learn something new about yourself.

EMOTIONAL ANOREXIA: INTIMACY STARVED

Even if you have never personally known anyone with the eating disorder anorexia nervosa, you most likely know what it is. You might not know all the specifics—irrational fear of weight gain, distorted body image, and restrictive eating habits—but you could probably identify an image of a frail, undernourished, and skeletal body and face as that of an anorexic. The problem with emotional anorexia, as I am calling intimacy issues, is that it can be difficult to recognize at the beginning of a relationship. Emotional anorexics crave intimacy and loving relationships; sometimes they are even very romantic and shower you with gifts as they relentlessly pursue you. But very similar to the commitmentphobe, they fear it and are usually incapable of maintaining it.

So what is emotional intimacy? Real intimacy takes time to establish. It involves trust and mutually feeling safe to be vulnerable, allowing healthy self-disclosure without fearing being betrayed or misunderstood. It involves respect, tolerance, and always sharing how you feel—no secrets. In a truly intimate relationship, you will feel safe, loved, appreciated, and emotionally supported. Emotional intimacy is about knowing the good, the bad, the silly, and the ugly and loving each other anyway, unconditionally. It's about having each other's backs. A well-balanced meal can never be achieved without real intimacy.

Emotional anorexics fear real intimacy. Some have no problem making commitments, as long as you don't ask them to reveal their true self or talk about their deepest feelings, or be good at supporting you. Others are terrified of being engulfed and will create distance and flee as soon as any real intimacy is achieved.

White Bread

Fresh white bread is really tasty. Personally I like a crusty French baguette or an Italian loaf, sometimes Tuscan or *ciabatta*. But as anyone who has tried to eat healthy knows, there is little to no nutritional value in white bread. It's full of empty calories. Dating someone who's emotionally unavailable is a lot like eating white bread.

When you are in a relationship with an emotionally unavailable person, you will likely notice the following things:

- She will keep a lot of secrets and have overdeveloped boundaries.

- You may feel like you don't truly know each other.

- You'll rarely, if ever, get invited to her place. She'll prefer to come to yours so she can control when to leave.

- Getting her on the phone or getting to see her will happen only sporadically.

- The simple, mundane details of her life will be a mystery; don't expect her to show interest in yours.

- You probably won't meet her family, and she'll resist having to spend time with yours.

- When you have sex, it's just sex; it's passionate, but doesn't involve intimately connecting and making love.

Emotionally unavailable people are protecting their heart. They create barriers to keep others at a safe distance so that they can feel safe. They create a false front to hide their inner feelings: the pain of having been hurt or the fear of being hurt—many times both.

If the pattern-identifying exercise at the beginning of this chapter revealed that you're attracted to emotionally unavailable people, you have to explore why that is. You are probably somewhat unavailable yourself. Someone who is truly emotionally available isn't interested in someone who is unavailable. If you have been through a recent breakup or other difficult time, then temporarily being emotionally unavailable is understandable, even necessary. It's wise to take time to heal, self-reflect, and hopefully grow. But if a past traumatic event or heartbreak is causing you to fear being hurt again, it is going to require some courage to open your heart to find true love. If you never learned how to be emotionally available as a child, you'll have to decide if you're willing to try now.

To be emotionally available is to be willing to offer your whole self and to explore and accept your partner's whole self. If your heart rate is starting to go up and you're feeling uncomfortable at just the thought of doing that, then take a few deep breaths. Any kind of change is always a process, so don't pressure yourself to become emotionally available overnight. You can do it in small steps, one day at a time.

Actions to Become More Emotionally Available

1. Decide you want to be emotionally available. Everything we do is a choice, whether that choice is conscious or not. Happiness is a choice, sadness is a choice, forgiveness is a choice, and so on. Make a conscious choice to be more open. Choose to be willing to reveal personal details about yourself to someone you care about and would like to get closer to. You don't have to actually do it yet; for now just decide that you're willing to try.

2. Get in touch with yourself. Before you can share your feelings, you have to know what they are.

- Make some quiet time alone to reflect. Turn off the TV and all other distractions.

- Allow yourself to recognize and name what you're feeling. Are you angry or sad; are you scared?

- Don't judge what you're feeling, just acknowledge it.

- Learn how to meditate; it will help you get in touch with your inner self.

- Write your feelings in your personal journal.

Many people become emotionally unavailable because they fear their emotions may be overwhelming if they try to explore and acknowledge their deepest feelings. But those feelings are only thoughts. Thoughts are manageable if you're willing to believe they are. Keeping things suppressed causes them to fester and become worse. If you can't do this by yourself, ask a mentor or trusted friend if you can share your thoughts with him or her. Or find a good therapist. Most of what a therapist does is listen—confidentially, without bias or judgment. I promise you that if you let your feelings out, you'll be very thankful that you did.

3. Trust yourself. Trusting others is not as important as trusting yourself. You can never control what someone else does. People are human, and even the best people sometimes make mistakes and hurt us. The only person you can absolutely trust is you.

- Trust yourself to be able to handle whatever comes your way.

- Promise yourself you will always nurture yourself and take care of your own needs.

- Promise yourself you will be emotionally strong no matter what. If you are unable to fulfill that promise by yourself, promise yourself you'll get professional help.

- Trust yourself to make well-thought-out choices.

When you truly trust yourself, you will be able to trust others; because if they do fail you, you'll know you will be okay.

4. Allow yourself to be emotionally vulnerable. Being vulnerable does not mean being weak. It actually takes an emotionally strong person to allow himself or herself to be vulnerable. I know it can be scary. If you reveal your true self and feelings, there is a chance you can get hurt. You could be rejected or misunderstood. But you could also achieve real intimacy, and love like you have never known it before.

> With great risk comes great reward. Great love can only exist if you allow yourself to be emotionally vulnerable.

5. Share yourself with your partner. Mutually share your deepest feelings, goals, and fears. If you get fearful, ask a question. Listening to your partner's truths may give you confidence to reciprocate with your own. Share something you have never revealed about yourself before. It may be scary at first, but as your partner learns more about you and loves you anyway, it will become increasingly easy to just be yourself. You can each be yourself together.

6. Spend quality time together. Cuddling on the couch and watching a movie is nice, but it doesn't foster communication. Do some things together that are less about the *doing* and more about being with each other. Take a walk or hike, go out to eat, or take a drive without music (at least turn it down), and use that time to share your thoughts and feelings.

7. Be patient and keep looking forward. Change is always a process. Take it slow and allow a new habit to gradually develop as you regularly check in with yourself to identify what you're feeling. Continue to reveal your feelings to your partner. Utilize the healthy communication guidelines in chapter 1, "No Pressure Cookers," page 24.

Now that you know what it takes to achieve emotional intimacy, require it from your all romantic relationships. That's not to say you should try to change someone who is emotionally unavailable. You can't. By allowing yourself to be emotionally available, you'll be able to judge another's availability. It takes wisdom and some practice to know when to reveal things about yourself and how much to reveal in a new relationship. The "Healthy Boundaries" section in chapter 7, on page 175, will help you set a healthy pace. Make a choice to let go of any partner who doesn't welcome, embrace, and return your healthy vulnerability. Anyone who doesn't appreciate your emotional intimacy doesn't deserve your physical intimacy. Chapter 3 will help you prevent sex from clouding your choices.

Devastating Disorders

There are two dating disorders that are extremely difficult to cure, if they can be cured at all. I want you to recognize the characteristics so that if you start dating someone with either, you can save yourself the heartache and frustration and get out quickly. I'm speaking about narcissistic and borderline personality disorders.

Yo-Yo Dieting

Falling in love with someone with borderline personality disorder (BPD) is like yo-yo dieting—for both of you. Those with BPD desperately fear abandonment and crave intimacy. They will seek out a deeply intimate connection. They usually lack boundaries and quickly idealize a person who gives them special attention. For the non-BP partner, presumably you, finding such an intense, loving connection makes you feel safe—appreciated and wanted. But for the BP, feeling that vulnerable is frightening. So as soon as intimacy is achieved, she will subconsciously find fault with you. She'll push you away, create drama, and be argumentative, and she will make it out to be all your fault. She will leave you or cause you to leave; either way, you will be devastated and confused. But as soon as distance is achieved, the BP will feel desperately abandoned again. She'll rush back to you, behaving as the original person you fell in love with. Relieved, you'll take her back into your loving arms—but the cycle is just starting all over again. On again, off again, on again—just like yo-yo dieting.

Here are some things to keep in mind about people with borderline personality disorder:

- They flip-flop back and forth between feeling abandoned and feeling engulfed and overwhelmed.

- There is no gray area; their thinking is strictly black-and-white.

- Their fear of abandonment is so intense that they will always abandon you before you can abandon them.

- On some level they know they have issues, so they can't trust anyone who could care about them.

- The closer you get, the more they act out.

- They frequently create conflict to heighten the intensity of the relationship so they can feel more loved.

If you are in a relationship where you feel like you're constantly walking on eggshells and you just aren't sure what you do that makes your lover turn on you, she may have BPD. You could be just about perfect—swearing eternal devotion, being supportive, loving, and understanding—but a BP can never feel safe. She can never allow herself to be vulnerable. As soon as it feels like you're close again, she will pull away. This has nothing to do with you; don't allow her to make you insecure or doubt yourself. Something as simple as not answering your cell phone on the first ring can cause a BP to feel abandoned. BPs live in the present moment and demand constant attention. If you need a minute alone or even just drift into your thoughts, they feel that you're abandoning them, and they will attack. Yo-yo dieting is extremely unhealthy.

- Borderline personality disorder is exceptionally difficult to cure.

- You cannot help a BP.

- You cannot reason with a BP.

- Your love will never be enough to make a BP happy.

- Cut your losses now. Move on. Put yourself first.

- You deserve someone who can genuinely accept your love.

BPD was previously thought to only occur in women. But psychology has proved men do suffer from it too.

Nausea and Dehydration

Do you remember the very public divorce of Christie Brinkley and Peter Cook? From the outside looking in, they had seemed to have it all: stunning beauty, two gorgeous children, fame, fortune, philanthropy, and a Hamptons/Hollywood lifestyle. But their life behind closed doors was a different story. Christie's very handsome husband publicly admitted to having an affair and lying. After a court psychologist diagnosed him with narcissistic personality disorder (NPD), he even publicly admitted that. In true narcissistic style, he loved the public attention. He tried to preserve his inflated ego by depicting Christie as the villain. It was a very nasty, nauseating battle.

Narcissism is extreme self-absorption. A narcissist doesn't feel empathy, so it is impossible for a narcissist to achieve real intimacy with anyone. Outward appearances are important to narcissists. They usually have tremendously high self-confidence and put themselves on a pedestal above everyone else. They belittle those they view as inferior and expect everyone to always go along with them. But they suffer from fragile self-esteem. They don't handle criticism well, and within a relationship they commonly become manipulative, controlling, and unfaithful. They can even become abusive.

Unfortunately, some pretty amazing women have fallen for narcissists. Narcissists envy those they perceive as nearly perfect. In the beginning they can be very seductive and witty. They are also typically very charismatic, attractive, and charming people. It's easy to fall for a narcissist. But once you do, don't count on living happily ever after. He's not capable of truly caring for you. He will dehydrate you, as you'll give more than you take in. Since narcissists are not capable of emotional intimacy, they usually can't sustain a relationship for very long. If they do, their partner feels incredibly lonely. They love to stroke their own ego. They frequently jump from one relationship to the next. Following are the signs to look for before you get too caught up in a narcissist's serving of egocentricity.

Narcissistic Personality Disorder Checklist:

____ He talks about himself and monopolizes the conversation.

____ He never asks about me, or never listens when he does.

____ He exaggerates his achievements or talents; acts boastful or conceited.

____ He expects constant praise or adoration.

____ He disregards or diminishes my feelings.

____ He's demanding of me but isn't there for me.

____ He puts himself first.

____ He has a sense of entitlement and becomes angry if not treated specially.

____ He's easily hurt and easily feels rejected; he can't handle criticism.

____ He has a fragile self-esteem but high self-confidence.

____ He thinks others are jealous of him.

____ He envies others who are successful, attractive, or stylish.

____ He takes advantage of others for his own gain.

____ He wants to have the best of everything and is materialistic.

Some people possess various narcissistic tendencies without having NPD. But if you can check off five or more statements above, you are dating a narcissistic personality. Get out now! There is no hope for improvement. People with NPD are rarely changed even a little bit—and that is if they even want help, which most of them don't, as they think they're perfect.

Don't fool yourself into thinking there is any hope. Save yourself now; just move on.

Narcissism is more common in men but can affect women too.

Ingredients vs. Presentation

Self-esteem and self-confidence frequently get mistaken for one another, but they are two separate things. Self-confidence is the belief in one's ability to do something, such as managing a business, speaking in public, playing sports, or even making friends. Self-esteem is how one feels about oneself; one's inner dialog. It is incredibly common for very successful people to have high self-confidence but very low self-esteem. The self-confidence masks their feelings of inadequacy.

Doggie Bag

Dating Disorders

➡ **Face your fears.** Unacknowledged fears and unhealed issues are what sabotage relationships. Recognize and face your fears to avoid future dating disasters.

➡ **Discover and break your relationship pattern.** Until you recognize and then break your pattern, you will continue to choose the same kind of partners and your relationships will continue to fail.

➡ **Commit to your personal junk-food and healthy-meal flags.** Decide what you truly want and what behaviors and characteristics will work best for you in your next relationship.

➡ **Commitment issues are very common.** If your good relationship suddenly ended or turned bad, there is a good possibility that fear of commitment was the cause. You may have passive commitment issues too.

➡ **You can't force someone to love you.** If your lover has said good-bye, you have to gracefully let him go. Acknowledge his feelings and take good care of yourself.

➡ **Push the pause button.** When you feel angry, rejected, hurt, or revengeful, stop! Don't do anything but breathe. Breathe deeply and think of something positive you can do for yourself.

➡ **Change your perception.** Feeling rejected? Change your perception. Find the cons of the relationship and decide for yourself that *you* don't want her.

➡ **Keep your thoughts in the present.** Don't look backward or forward; keep your thoughts on what you can do right now, for you. Stay in reality; fantasies can be very destructive. Stop running the highlight reel of all the good times.

➡ **Create a new habit.** A big part of breaking up is breaking the habit of being with the other person. Create new positive habits for yourself.

➡ **When you chase something, it runs.** Allow a potential partner the space to come to you. When you put too much "must have" on something you only push it away.

➡ **With great risk comes great reward.** You cannot achieve emotional intimacy without allowing yourself to be vulnerable. Real emotional intimacy is the foundation of true love.

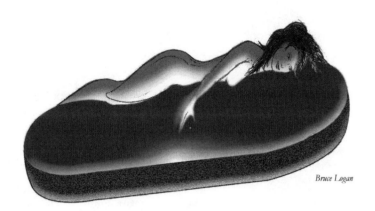

Bruce Logan

CHAPTER THREE

Comfort Food Overindulgence

There are many reasons you may reach for comfort food. Perhaps you're feeling lonely, emotional, or stressed out, or maybe you're having a craving. Or you may just simply be hungry because you waited too long to eat. No matter why you choose to indulge in comfort food, isn't the intention always to make you feel better?

Yet depending on what kind of comfort food you choose and how much you devour, the actual comfort achieved may be fleeting. You may continue to consume more and more, all the while craving that warm and fuzzy sensation. But feelings of guilt or regret do ultimately follow.

Sex can be an awful lot like comfort food. In the moment, it's all about pleasure. It's hot, fun, and yummy—sometimes even decadent— and the consequences are far from any present concern. But when it's over, you might not be left feeling comfortable. You may even feel a lot worse. If you overindulge in comfort food without any healthy meals, you can even become depressed.

Your choices about sex have a profound effect on your self-esteem and your relationships. Sex can be wonderful, empowering, and healthy. Sex can be considered making love. Sex can also be destructive, unhealthy, and obsessive. It can keep you addicted to an unhealthy situation. And if you confuse all sex for love, you most certainly won't be feeling comforted.

Take the following quiz to find out if sex is making you unhealthy.

Quiz: Is Comfort Food Making You Unhealthy?

Take this quiz according to the choices you typically make about sex.

_____ 1. You're on a first date, and you're really connecting. What do you do next?

A.) That doesn't happen to me often, so I end up having sex.

B.) I stay out late (or up all night) and drink a little too much, but we only make out and don't have sex.

C.) I'm a little shy and don't know how to show her I like her.

D.) I let my date know that I like her and just kiss her goodnight.

_____ 2. It's midnight, and the hot meal you're crazy about calls out of the blue. What do you do?

A.) I don't answer the phone.

B.) I answer but only talk; I don't let him come over.

C.) We have phone sex. (This may include sexting.)

D.) I invite him over, possibly go out for a drink, and we have great sex.

____ 3. Your boyfriend or girlfriend broke up with you. What happens to your relationship?

A.) We remain friends and still occasionally have sex.

B.) She's dating other people, but I only have sex with her.

C.) I'm trying to let go, and I'm moving on with my life.

D.) We're both dating other people but still hook up with each other.

____ 4. The hot meal you're dating asks you to text some sexy pictures. How do you respond?

A.) I text him naked pictures that don't show my face.

B.) I tell him I'm not comfortable texting things like that.

C.) I text him close-ups of my genitals and breasts.

D.) I text him pictures of me in sexy clothes.

____ 5. What's *most* important to you in a potential partner?

A.) How hot she is. Looks and chemistry are most important.

B.) How much I enjoy her company.

C.) How much she likes me.

D.) How much we have in common.

____ 6. We had sex for the first time

A.) on our first date.

B.) on our second or third date.

C.) on our fourth through seventh date.

D.) on our eighth date or after.

____ 7. After we had sex,

A.) we got closer and started spending more time together.

B.) we saw a lot of each other, but it ended within three months.

C.) he occasionally called for drinks and sex but not much more.

D.) he never called, and I never saw him again.

____ 8. If I'm not happy with the way my meal is treating me,

A.) I stop having sex with him until we get back on track.

B.) I stay with him for the sexual chemistry. I don't find that very often.

C.) if talking doesn't fix things, I leave him.

D.) I use sex to get him to do what I want.

____ 9. You're angry at your meal. What happens next?

A.) She initiates sex before we finish talking about the issue.

B.) I talk to her about the issue, and then we have great make-up sex.

C.) I show her I'm angry with my actions, including aggressive sex.

D.) I don't see her for a while until I calm down.

____ 10. You're dating and sleeping with a hot meal, and you start to see some junk-food flags. How do you handle this?

A.) I put up with the bad things because the rest is so good.

B.) I talk to him about my concerns so he can change.

C.) I guard my feelings and try not to get too attached.

D.) I end the relationship so I can find someone healthy.

Using the key below, assign a score to each of your answers.

For questions 1 & 6:	For questions 2 & 7:	For questions 3 & 8:
A = 0	A = 5	A = 3
B = 1	B = 3	B = 0
C = 3	C = 1	C = 5
D = 5	D = 0	D = 1

For Questions 4 & 9:   For Questions 5 & 10:

For Questions 4 & 9:	For Questions 5 & 10:
A = 1	A = 0
B = 5	B = 3
C = 0	C = 1
D = 3	D = 5

Enter your score on the line below.

My Total Score _____

> One of my favorite sayings is "Sex makes you stupid," meaning that if you have sex before you really know who someone is, then you run the risk of getting hooked on the sex and ignoring all the junk-food flags he or she might be waving. When you're in lust, you're more likely to put up with bad behavior. If it begins with sex, then he may end up only using you as a sex buddy, satisfying his sexual needs but not letting you in emotionally. He gets what he wants, but you don't get what you want. Frequently, the potential of a relationship ends prematurely because one party loses interest after getting laid—and the other is left wanting more.

What Your Score Means

Use the guide below to determine if you're allowing sex to make you stupid.

If you scored 44–50, you're making smart choices about sex!

If you scored 30–43, you're making some smart choices, but you could sharpen your taste buds a little. If you're just looking to have fun, then there is nothing wrong with a little comfort food. But if you're looking for a real relationship, you need to use a little willpower when making your choices. Healthy food truly does make you feel better than comfort food.

If you scored 12–29, sex is spoiling your choices. When you overindulge in comfort food, your palate becomes contaminated; healthy food then just doesn't taste as good and isn't satisfying. You need to strengthen your boundaries so you can be more nutritious.

If you scored 0–12, sex is causing you to make stupid choices. This chapter is for you. Don't allow junk-food to make you unhealthy. Choose to be nutritious!

Why You Can't Give the Milk Away

Men's and women's brains have different chemical mixes. The younger the guy, the more sex is the primary goal on his mind—literally, as testosterone and vasopressin hormones are flooding his brain. Women have oxytocin flooding their brains. Oxytocin is the hormone that makes us feel all warm and fuzzy in romantic situations.[19] Since women have high levels of oxytocin all the time, they enjoy cuddling, talking, holding hands, and sex; but sex isn't always the main attraction. The only time a man experiences the highly pleasurable effects of oxytocin is in a burst at the moment of orgasm.

Bruce Logan

What all these chemical differences mean is that when a woman has sex with a man on the first or second date, his brain reaches its goal and achieves that desirable burst of oxytocin. His chemical levels then return to normal. He may not be interested enough to pursue her again, regardless of how he was acting preorgasm. Meanwhile, the woman's brain turns on super high oxytocin levels, and she definitely wants more. If she never hears from him again, cortisol (the stress hormone) starts to fill her brain, and she feels heartbroken. She may possibly even become depressed.

---

[19] Dr. Laura Berman on *The Oprah Winfrey Show,* "Behind Closed Doors: Sex Therapy," November 4, 2008.

A woman's self-esteem increases when she delays bringing sex into a new relationship. When she draws out the courting process, allowing affection and foreplay without consenting to intercourse, she feels powerful. Simultaneously, the man's brain has time to grow emotional attachment to her. Men who are ready for a relationship will take the time to get to know a woman. They'll respect her and desire her even more.

Kissing will never again be as passionate and romantic as it is before sex, so take your time and enjoy the anticipation it creates. Think about how amazing your first time is going to be when you're already falling in love. But if your date is only looking for casual sex, he'll reveal himself by being impatient and trying to rush you. That's a major junk-food flag. Don't let him manipulate you. He'll probably just stop calling. Be strong. You'll have just saved yourself a lot of potential anguish.

I'm not saying that sleeping with someone on the first date automatically means you have low self-esteem. I'm not saying that your lover can't be crazy about you and end up being *the one*. I'm just saying that that is definitely the exception. It's not what men and women are biologically programmed to do.

Of course, as men get older, they produce less testosterone, so they can control their sexual urges better—especially if they've reached an age where they're looking for a long-term, loving relationship. If you're both mature and you've discussed your life goals and you're both on the same page, trust your instincts. Sex with someone you're crazy about, who's also crazy about you, is one of the best things in life. Just don't go there until you know for sure that your partner *is* crazy about you. Make sure that that amazing chemistry is backed up with real feelings and that he or she is a well-balanced meal.

Midnight Snacks

At times, nothing tastes better than a midnight snack. When you're out having fun, it's common to work up a hunger. Many diners and drive-throughs do substantial business just after the bars' last call. Similarly, when you're sitting at home bored, lonely, or hyperactive, the fridge becomes a source of pleasure. Just like when the hot meal you're crazy about contacts you at the last minute for a booty call.

An occasional midnight snack or booty call is fun. It can certainly satisfy a craving. But it becomes a problem if you continually indulge at midnight. You don't want to mess up a healthy diet.

Part of the reason it's highly important to delay bringing sex into a new relationship is that you teach people how to treat you. If you show a meal that you don't value your sexuality by giving it up easily, then he won't value you either. However, he may enjoy the sex. If that's the case, he won't waste his time and money wining and dining you. He doesn't need to if you're willing to let him cut right to the chase. I'm not only speaking to women in this section. Some women use men for sex too, especially when they're pining for someone else.

I had a client whom I'll call Kelly. Kelly met a guy she really liked while she was out with friends one night. They seemed to really connect, and when her friends left, she stayed with him and his friends. They played pool and continued to drink until the bar closed. It was going really well, so she agreed to go home with him. They had amazing sex. But after that he never took her on a real date. He'd only invite her out for late-night drinks, after which they'd have great sex—frequently after he'd had dinner with a client or someone else. He was using her as a midnight snack. Many times he didn't even take her for drinks; it evolved into her just meeting him at his place. Kelly came to me to find out how she could turn it into a relationship. She desperately wanted to recapture what they had that first night. Unfortunately, it was too late. You can never go backward. She tried making him dinner and inviting him to parties; he was conveniently never available. For Kelly, the whole situation was less than convenient.

People do what they want to do. If you always remind yourself of that, it really is quite simple. As caring beings, we usually like to give people the benefit of the doubt. We frequently conjure up pleasant scenarios to explain away undesirable behavior: "he's really busy at work," "she's exhausted," "he's got a lot on his mind," "she's not ready"—you know what I'm talking about. These are rationalizations our friends help us come up with so we can feel okay about putting up with bad behavior. Regardless of how busy, tired, or distracted anyone is, people do what they want to do. You do what you want to do, right?

Kelly wanted to have sex with the guy she met. So she did. Even on his terms. Even after I suggested she stop having sex with him to see if he wanted to just spend time with her. I believe she didn't control her appetite because she already knew that answer and didn't like it. If he wanted to spend time with her, he would have taken her out to dinner or invited her out with his friends; he would have allowed the relationship to progress. All he wanted was sex.

As it turned out, Kelly had been trying to get a past boyfriend back. So in the meantime she was having fun partying and having casual hook-ups. Consequently, when she met someone interesting, it felt natural to get right into the sex. But he lost respect for her, or more likely he never had time to develop any respect, so all he saw was a midnight snack.

You have to know what you're looking for and then act according to what you ultimately want. If you truly do not want a relationship and you're just looking to have fun, then do whatever you want. Just don't expect more. If you truly do want a well-balanced meal to last long-term, then you have to be smart about sex. You have to control your appetite. Most importantly, you need to be honest with yourself. If the reason you don't want a relationship is that you're waiting for someone to come back, then you're sabotaging yourself. Don't put your life on hold to wait for a past love who isn't giving you what you want! I can assure you that will prevent you from ever having what you want.

Many clients come to me who are actively dating and having frequent midnight snacks while they're still in love with and pining for someone they can't have or can only periodically have. While they're craving that specific snack, they turn away or sabotage other potentially healthy meals and jump at any opportunity to satisfy their true craving. But remember, you teach people how to treat you. What the object of your desire learns is that he can have whatever he wants. So when he gets a late-night craving, all he has to do is pick up the phone—and usually just send a text. For him, it's a satisfying snack. All it really does for you is deprive you of substantial nutrients and leave you hungry. Leaving the door open to an unavailable love provides potent ingredients for unhealthy midnight snacks.

If you're just looking to have fun, then go ahead and indulge in all the midnight snacks you want. But if you truly want a relationship, be warned that midnight snacks are destructive to your diet. When you indulge in a midnight snack with significant meaning, the deprivation pains that follow can be debilitating. The next section will tell you what to do with those leftovers.

Leftovers

Any relationship expert, even anyone who has been single for a long time, can tell you that most new relationships last only three to six months. They start hot and heavy, and then one partner is usually left wondering what happened, while the other one is already on to the next.

Bruce Logan

There is a full menu of reasons this happens. (See chapter 2, "Dating Disorders," page 58, to read about the most common reasons.) For the one holding the leftovers, it's always painfully confusing.

The problem with food leftovers is that they are rarely as good as the original meal. When food is hot and fresh, and you're really enjoying it but you've eaten all that you can, it usually seems like a good idea to take some home for later. The next day you're full of anticipation as you prepare to enjoy it again. But it never tastes as satisfying the second time, does it? Sometimes it's still good. It's just different. It's colder, mushier, or maybe there just isn't enough left. The end result usually isn't fulfilling. The only way to achieve that initial culinary bliss is to go get another fresh meal.

Well, the same principle applies to romantic leftovers. When you feel connected with someone, you want more. If she doesn't want to be with you anymore, you're left with whatever she's willing to give you. If you choose to starve yourself waiting for whatever crumbs she may drop, you most certainly won't get the nutrition you need or deserve. When you do get the opportunity to indulge in your favorite leftover, it's never as good as it was originally. Physically it may be good, but mentally you will most likely feel worse when it's finished and gone again.

If you're indulging in leftovers right now, I'm hoping you can see what I'm trying to illustrate. I know you feel like you will never be as connected to anyone else as you are to this partner. I know no one else makes you feel like he does when you're with him. But someone else might not make you feel as lonely and empty as you feel when you're not with him. Someone else might truly love you and make you feel loved. I promise you this: you will never find someone else that you connect with as much as you do with this leftover as long as you are still allowing him to be a part of your life. You *will* find someone else if you're brave enough to let go of this leftover. I promise you!

> If the leftover you crave was all you ever got to eat, could you survive?

Imagine what would happen to your body if you only ate once or twice a month or less. Would you get the nutrients you need? Would you feel good? Would you look your best? Would eating only once or twice a month even make sense? And only junk food at that! If you are with a leftover, I want you to put a nutritional value on the amount of time you spend with him. If you couldn't survive on him, then throw him out! He has gone bad. He will never again be the person you fell in love with, and you're too good to wait around and rot while he's out having fun!

If you think you'll stop seeing him when you meet someone else, I'm telling you that will never happen. I see this all the time. If you're saying you do get out and date but you like your leftover best, the truth is that you are not truly open to anyone but him. You're pushing everyone else away. Energy is contagious, and as long as your energy is focused on a leftover, you will never attract a healthy meal. I promise you.

Ordering Online

I've heard people say about online dating, "By the time you meet, it's really just about whether you want to have sex or not." I find a lot of truth in that. You've seen each other's picture, exchanged e-mails, probably talked on the phone, and already know you have a lot in common. On paper you seem to work, and

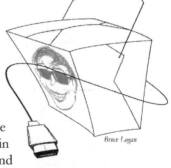

Bruce Logan

you feel some sort of a connection. The last piece of the puzzle is whether there's physical chemistry or not. How many times have you thought, "I hope she's as good in person!"? So if the attraction is there when you finally do meet, it's easy to feel comfortable with a virtual stranger. The pace of a relationship that begins on the Internet can become much accelerated. It can be wonderful, and it has resulted in marriage for a lot of couples. I just want you to keep in mind that you don't know the other person yet. You need to take some time to verify that everything she said in her profile is true and that she's as interested in you as you are in her.

Having met on the Internet adds a whole new dimension to beginning a relationship. You're essentially competing with all the other men or women on the website. You probably had conversations or e-mails, and maybe even dates, going with more than one person, so you'd better believe your meal did too. Just because you met doesn't mean your meal has stopped communicating with all the others. They possibly still have other dates lined up. Internet dating opens you up to many potential partners. You both can and should be very picky if you decide to date online. That's why it's even more important not to have sex right away. Ladies, you have to stroke his ego and make him *want* to wait for you. Let him show off a little and let him impress you. Gentleman, you have to make her or him feel cherished and respected. Most people need to feel needed. They need lots of acknowledgment that you like them. While you're not giving them sex, you need to give them everything else that they need. Make sure you tell them how much you enjoy their company. Never criticize them. Be affectionate (but not a tease) and ask them to be patient with you. Know without a doubt that you are worth waiting for! Then they'll know it, too.

Sexting

I have one suggestion about sexting—don't do it! I know it can be a big turn-on, and I know it can be fun. But sexting is dangerous fun. The consequences can be disastrous. If you are engaging in sexting, you're extending a lot of trust. Has that trust been earned? Are you assuming those pictures are for your partner's eyes only? If they're on his or her phone, the temptation to show you off just might be too inviting for him or her to pass up. Are you sure you want to be a pin-up for all his or her friends? And if you have never actually met a person, but you've only met online, then never engage in sexting! If you make your connection all about sex, you will never get more than that. Most importantly, women should never initiate sexting with a man. He may not approve, and it can make him lose all interest in you. You can be assured it will lower his respect for you. Do you want to be the girl he sexualizes, or do you want to become the love of his life? Sex is not the way to a man's heart.

If you're in a committed, loving relationship, enjoying a well-balanced meal, taking sexy pictures can be fun. But be smart about where those pictures are kept.

Feast or Famine

When the sex works in a relationship, meaning it's healthy, consensual, frequent, and fulfilling, then it only makes up 10 percent of the overall relationship. But when the sex doesn't work, meaning there isn't any, it's not satisfying, or one partner wants more than the other, then it becomes 90 percent of the relationship. Sex is the connection that bonds you together, or it's the problem that can tear you apart.

Why is sex only 10 percent of the relationship when it's good? It's because other elements of the relationship, the components of true love, are the most important. (See the relationship pyramid on page 200) However, those good things can begin to unravel without the "glue" of a mutually satisfying sexual relationship. There is a sense of disconnection when one or both partners feel frustrated, and this frustration spills over into other aspects of the relationship. It's hard to feel loving and compassionate toward someone who isn't meeting your needs. I have heard some women say that as soon as her man put a ring on her finger, she didn't have to have sex anymore. Even if they don't admit it, there are a lot of women who feel the same way. I feel that is manipulative. Sex is an important part of a healthy relationship. Without sex, you're really just friends. The reason marriage gets a bad rap is lack of sex. Don't let that happen to your relationship!

If you don't genuinely enjoy sex or find yourself avoiding it, then perhaps you should seek out a sex therapist that can help you discover how wonderful it can be. If you usually do enjoy sex, then even when you think you're not in the mood, think again. Your thoughts create your feelings. Open your mind and allow your partner to get you in the mood; I bet you'll actually enjoy it.

Just about every man that I have coached at one point has asked, "Is it shallow that what she looks like is really important to me?" "No," I always say, "your brain is designed to function that way." A brain-imaging study of men in love revealed that their visual processing center is what triggers their passion.[20] That's why men are visually stimulated by sexy pictures, lingerie, and even pornography. It is not shallow; it's how they're biologically programed to be stimulated. If you are a man, I hope that helps you feel validated.

If you are a woman, you need to know how important your appearance is to your man. Once you get comfortable in a relationship, it's easy to lose focus on keeping the physical attraction alive. When you look at your man, the cognitive centers, not the visual centers, are what activate in your brain. You get comfortable and frequently start dressing in frumpy sweats and flannels when you're hanging around the house or in bed. He's not the center of your attention—or affection—anymore, but he needs to be. That's why many relationships go bad. Of course you can be comfortable, but make sure you still look cute—desirable. Something like boy shorts and a fitted T-shirt will drive him crazy. Ask him what he'd like to see you in.

Touch each other frequently. Make each other feel wanted. Hold hands, hug your partner from behind, and even pat his or her butt. Simple affection keeps the sexual connection between you alive. An active sex life can keep a couple happy for decades. Plus it's the fountain of youth! Great sex enjoyed on a regular basis can make you look seven to twelve years younger.[21] It makes your immune system 33 percent stronger, decreases your risk of heart disease by up to 50 percent, and reduces insomnia and stress. So if you're feeling too stressed out to have sex, maybe what you really need is a little more foreplay to get you in the mood. Communication is a big part of great sex. Guys, kiss her neck and ask her what she wants you to do to her. And girls, instead of saying no, tell him what you'd like him to do (even if he doesn't ask). It will totally turn him on. Oh, and the "I have a headache" excuse really doesn't fit either. Orgasms are a natural pain reliever. They can even relieve menstrual cramps.

Yet all this wonderful sex is still only 10 percent of a healthy relationship. When you first meet, sex is fun and exciting, and it's normal

---

[20]Daniel Goleman, "Desire: His and Hers," in *Social Intelligence: The New Science of Human Relationships* (New York: Bantam Books, 2006), 198.

[21]Dr. Laura Berman on *The Oprah Winfrey Show*, November 4, 2008, as viewed at http://www.oprah.com/relationships/Secrets-of-Sex-Therapy-How-to-Improve-Your-Sex-Life/2.

to feel like you can't get enough of each other. As the relationship moves forward, you should connect in other ways too. Discovering each other as individuals, talking, doing things, and going places together are the things that build a healthy relationship. I have to say it again: sex is not the way to a person's heart. Think of sex as the dessert to a healthy meal; it's highly enjoyable, but that's not where you get your nutrition.

So if you feel like sex is more than 50 percent of your connection, then it's not love; it's lust. You may even have a sexual addiction. Frequently, sex is used to mask or hide the real issues you need to discuss. Sexual intimacy is often confused for emotional intimacy. Do you feel like having sex is the only way for you to be loved? Perhaps you have nothing else in common with your partner and every time you see each other it's all about sex. Maybe sometimes you really don't even get along, which may be what makes it feel exciting. Make-up sex is always amazing, but that's supposed to be because you have resolved something and you are feeling closer.

If the above paragraph describes you and it feels like sex is a disproportionately large part of your relationships, it might be helpful for you to seek out a Sex and Love Addicts Anonymous (SLAA) meeting in your area. These meetings are free, and there are even some you can attend online. Visit www.slaafws.org for more information and to take their forty-question self-diagnosis quiz.

After the exciting beginning stage of a relationship is over, if your meal wants sex more than once a day on a daily basis, then he is probably a sex addict. If you're having a hard time keeping up but you don't want to lose him, gently suggest he attend an SLAA meeting. Offer to go with him. If he refuses, then it might be good for you to go on your own to see what it's all about. You can listen to other people's stories to help you decide if you'll be able to handle your relationship. With hope you'll see that if he isn't willing to work on his addiction, then you deserve better. Always love yourself first! If you have a hard time doing that, then Al-Anon meetings will be great for you. Visit www.al-anon.org. They focus primarily on people who love an alcoholic, but it's great for anyone who loves any type of addict.

If your man or woman frequently doesn't want to have sex or never wants to have sex, be gentle in how you talk to him or her about it. Pressuring your partner or making him or her feel inadequate will only worsen the situation. Women, if you approach your man about this subject with too much dominant energy, you'll emasculate him. Don't embarrass him by telling all your friends about it either! This goes for men too. This is a private issue between just the two of you. Assure your partner you love her, and make her feel safe to confide her feelings to you.

Ladies, if your man is going through a major financial difficulty or other stressful situation, it's very possible that his interest in sex will diminish. It has nothing to do with you! For many men, self-worth largely depends on career success. If your man is having career difficulties, give him emotional support and be patient. Let him be the one to initiate sex. Gentlemen, if you're going through a tough career or financial time, it's normal to lose interest in sex.

For the record, a great sex life doesn't have to mean having sex every day. It's perfectly normal to skip a day or two when life gets busy. Just set a goal to have it at least twice a week. Make an appointment for sex if you have to; schedule the day and time and give yourself something to look forward to. Send each other little notes in anticipation. Buy some lingerie to help you or your partner feel sexy. Share your fantasies and do some role-playing. Be creative, and make it exciting. The couple that plays together stays together—and lives long and happy lives.

Doggie Bag
Comfort Food Overindulgence

➡ **Be honest with yourself and define what you truly want.** Choose to act according to what you ultimately want, not what you want right now.

➡ **Don't allow sex to make you stupid.** Delay bringing sex into a relationship until you truly know who you're having sex with.

➡ **Midnight snacks can ruin your diet.** If all you want is sex, have as many booty calls as you want. But if you want a well-balanced meal, sex should not be the basis for why you see each other.

➡ **Don't indulge in leftovers.** Leave the past in the past so you can find true happiness.

➡ **Take Internet dating slowly.** Assume anyone you meet on the Internet is seeing other people. Slow the pace of becoming physically intimate.

➡ **Don't participate in sexting.** Never initiate it!

➡ **Sex is the glue that keeps a relationship solid.** When you find a well-balanced meal, make an effort to keep your sex life active and happy.

CHAPTER FOUR

Stop Playing With Your Food

When you were little, did you ever play with your food? Perhaps you pushed your mashed potatoes into shapes with your fork or arranged your peas in a line. Maybe you even flung them off your spoon at your sibling. Playing with your food may have made meals more interesting but certainly not more appetizing. Let's face it—manipulating your food was usually just a way to avoid eating it. But spreading it around to look like you ate it didn't usually fool your parents, did it?

Playing games in a relationship doesn't work either. Games create competition, and a winner and loser. Playing games is manipulative and a way to avoid intimacy. Some people think game playing does make things more interesting. It's considered cool if you have *game*. But interesting doesn't mean healthy. Game playing is usually a symptom of insecurity, fear, and immaturity. Nutritious adults don't sabotage their relationships by playing games.

Eat Your Veggies

Clients frequently ask me how long they should wait before responding to a text or phone call. The answer is, don't wait. The idea that you have to play hard-to-get is junk-food. If you begin a relationship by playing games of any kind, you will ultimately lose. Now having said that, playing hard-to-get may be required to get a player. But do you want a player? If so, be careful what you wish for. Players play because they're not looking for emotional intimacy. They're just looking for fun, so they play by their own rules. If you try to break their rules, there is no compromise; they just move on to play with another. If you opt to play, you have to be very careful with your heart. Players can be very exciting, but they are high-calorie junk-food. Wouldn't you rather have a well-balanced meal? A person who is looking for a well-balanced meal wants someone who is communicative.

I had a client whom I'll call Josh. When Josh came to me, he was dating eleven different girls. He'd met each one on the Internet. Despite how that sounds, Josh was not a player. He wasn't sleeping with any of them. He was desperately searching for a well-balanced meal to potentially make his wife. And he was a good catch. The girl he found most attractive, Carol, was perfectly his physical type. She had dark hair, green eyes, and a petite, athletic body. As established in the previous chapter, on page 118, men are visually stimulated. But she was playing hard-to-get. He'd leave her a message, and she'd call him back a few days later with her limited availability. In the meantime, he was arranging dates with girls who were available. Josh was a gentleman, so he would never cancel a confirmed date to accommodate another girl, even if he liked her better. Consequently, while he was waiting to get to know Carol better, he got to know Denise. Denise was tall and blonde, not really his preferred physical type. But in Josh's words, she was communicative. He said, "She always answers the phone when I call, and if I miss her, she calls me right back." He really liked that. And he started to really like her. He gave up on Carol and all the other girls. He made an exclusive commitment to Denise because she was the most communicative.

Real intimacy begins with communication. If you are looking for a truly intimate relationship, you have to communicate honestly. You still need to hold your boundaries, as you'll learn in chapter 7. And you should wait to start sexual intimacy. But you can respond to a communication as soon as you want. If a person is turned off by healthy communication, you don't want that person anyway.

Think of healthy communication as eating your veggies. Veggies are an important part of a well-balanced meal. There usually aren't many vegetables in junk food. So by simply eating your veggies, you may weed out a lot of players and potential junk-food.

For men: You are responsible for initiating communication. One of my male clients recently called because he hadn't heard from the girl he'd just spent the night with. He was confused as to whether she liked him or not. I asked if he had called or texted her. "No," he said, "I was waiting to hear from her first." "She's waiting to hear from you," I said. "You're the guy." He had no idea that he should make the first contact. I realize today's women are not exactly traditional, and many of them do make the first contact. I also know men now often give women their card and say "call me" instead of asking for their number. But that makes the woman the masculine energy. Unless you want a masculine energy woman who will always take the lead, be the man by taking the traditional lead in communication. This is especially the case after you have sex with a girl. Even if she initiated the sex, she will wait to hear from you afterward.

The above story about Josh also illustrates that physical attraction is very important, but it can't overpower bad behavior. Outward beauty diminishes quickly when you play games instead of being honest. On the other hand, good behavior increases physical attraction.

Juicing

Juicing is a quick and efficient way to consume lots of fruits and vegetables. It helps your body absorb nutrients better because it breaks them down into a more digestible form. Juicing is basically a shortcut to good nutrition. Many people, especially women, think they can juice a relationship. They test their new lover to see how he or she will respond in order to judge his or her nutritional value. The problem is that many foods don't respond well to being cut into pieces and pushed through a juicer. The manipulation changes their consistency, and they can become

125

pretty nasty. Then you have to throw out what might have been good for you if you had simply just let it be. It's a waste of healthy food. If you do it too much, you'll find yourself perpetually hungry—a.k.a. alone.

True love cannot exist without emotional intimacy. Respect and trust are two essential ingredients that allow vulnerability to develop. Without vulnerability, you cannot achieve emotional intimacy—true love. I know I'm repeating myself, but I believe this bears repeating in this chapter to help you understand how playing the testing game sabotages your chance at true love. You teach people how to treat you. When you test them, you teach them they can't trust you—that you're not genuine. Most tests involve creating a false situation to see how your lover will react or respond. The object is to test their character and observe how they truly handle themselves as opposed to how they might say they would. It sounds good in theory, but in reality it's manipulation. The test situation usually appears as drama from out of the blue to the receiver. It may make you appear overly or inappropriately emotional. It's confusing, and it suddenly depicts you in a different light—all junk-food flags to a healthy meal. Trust me; even if you get the desired response, you have changed your meal's perception of you—usually in a negative way, and sometimes irreparably. It may make you feel closer to your meal, but it will do the opposite for him or her. It doesn't matter if your meal passes if the test causes him or her to leave you. If your meal doesn't pass, that doesn't mean he or she wouldn't pass if the situation were real instead of contrived. A bad reaction is most likely caused by the test itself—and to you creating unnecessary drama.

The problem for some is that they don't consciously test their meal. They instinctually do it out of insecurity. This is particularly true of people who have abandonment issues. The fear of their partner leaving them motivates them to act out and behave badly to test if their lover will stay or go. But what this behavior usually accomplishes is pushing their meal away, as their meal becomes frustrated at all the dysfunction.

You have to create a habit of checking in with yourself when you feel insecure. The first question you should ask yourself is "Am I deciding for him how he feels?" When you think "He's tired of me" or "She's going to leave me" or "He doesn't really love me," you are deciding how your partner feels. Then you create a test to confirm your theory. However, you created the whole thing in your head. You don't know how he or she feels. If you feel insecure or fear abandonment, your perception is tainted. You need to keep your thoughts on you and what you're feeling, not what you're feeling about what your partner is feeling. You cannot control what he or she thinks, feels, or does. I know that can be frightening, but when you try to control, you lose control. You destroy the intimacy in the relationship. Push the pause button. Allow your partner to do what he or she wants to do. Be confident. Behave in an empowered way that will make your partner crazy about you, not a way that will drive him or her crazy. Chapter 7 will help you become empowered.

Stirring the Pot

One of the most damaging games you can play is intentionally flirting with another person to make your meal jealous. Both men and women can be very territorial. When you flirt with another, all you're doing is telling your girl or guy you don't care about his or her feelings—and of course that he or she can't trust you. Challenging the safety within your relationship destroys emotional intimacy. Plus, when you do so, you're playing with the emotions of the person you're flirting with, and you're leading that person on. It's mean to give someone false hope for your own selfish gain. Not to mention it can be dangerous. Either person may have a violent temper or jealous mate that you don't know about. You may create a physical fight. If you think it's cool to have men or women fight over you, your self-esteem needs a lot of improvement.

If you feel like you need more attention from your meal, then you need to inspire him to give you attention in a loving way—not through manipulation. The best way to change someone else is to change yourself and hopefully change the way he responds to you. Do something nice for him or her. Give him a positive reason to appreciate you. If you try showing your partner loving behavior and it doesn't get his attention, then get rid of him—he is junk-food. Intentionally destroying your intimate connection will never help a relationship. It may temporarily get your partner to pay more attention to you, but in the long run, you're destroying his feelings for you. Nobody will truly cherish a person he can't trust. He most definitely won't allow himself to be vulnerable to you.

Cracking Gum and Blowing Bubbles

The title "player" usually refers to men, but women can be players too. A player is a master of manipulation who only cares about himself or herself. Besides just eating your veggies, there are some other behaviors you can keep an eye out for to help you identify if a player is playing you.

1. He only communicates via text. If he arranges all your dates and only communicates by sending a text, he is avoiding intimacy. That's a good sign he's only looking for sexual interaction. A true connection cannot be established without personal interaction.

2. She disappears for days. Out of sight, out of mind. When she doesn't want you, you won't hear from her. But when she wants you, she'll turn on a mad flurry of communication. Players want immediate gratification. She'll rarely if ever make plans with you in advance; everything will be last-minute. Don't give in to it. If she can't wait, she doesn't really want *you*. You're just someone to fill her current need.

3. His words are empty. Actions speak louder than words. Does he talk about things he wants to do and then never follow through? He probably does want to do those things, just not necessarily with you. Does he tell you all the things you want to hear and then seem to forget what he said? People do what they want to do, but players will say whatever they think will get them what they want. Listen to their actions, not their words. Don't make excuses for bad behavior.

4. Her life away from you is vague. She probably has several other relationships going, so she won't want to tell you details about her schedule. She won't want to tell you about past relationships either; there are probably too many, and some may still be happening.

5. He makes you feel like the center of his world. When you're together he's incredibly attentive and only focused on you. He's smooth and knows all the right things to say. But how is he when you're not together? If his behavior changes drastically, it's because someone else is the center of his world. There are probably a handful of other girls who think they're the center of his world some nights too.

Between-Meal Snacks

When your stomach is growling out loud and your next meal is nowhere in sight, it's common to reach for a between-meal snack. Depending on what you choose to consume, a snack can be quite filling and even satisfying. But it usually lacks the necessary nutrition to be considered a well-balanced meal. More often than not, after a little time passes, you find yourself feeling hungry again. Rebound relationships are pretty much the same as between-meal snacks.

As I mentioned in the "Hunger Pains" section of chapter 2, on page 75, the easiest way to break a habit is to replace it with something else—or someone else, when you're trying to alleviate the pain of a breakup. For people who suffer from abandonment issues or love addiction, the fear of never finding love again can be avoided if you love again right away. A new relationship can be exciting and much more fun than licking your wounds alone. Rebound sex releases all those wonderful chemicals in your brain that can help heal your broken heart. Be careful that what you're feeling isn't a fantasy. Be aware that any deep connection or loving feelings you're experiencing are not real—at least not yet; it's too soon. If you share them with your snack, you are playing games with your snack's feelings. Rebound relationships usually lead to heartbreak for the between-meal snack.

Audrey had gone through an extremely painful breakup with Eddie, whom she considered the love of her life. Both of them had agreed it was the best relationship they had ever had, and she truly believed they were going to be married. Unfortunately, Eddie had commitment issues that had never surfaced before, and after struggling with his anxiety for two years, it caused him to destroy their incredible connection. Audrey was devastated and didn't date again for two years. She couldn't accept that Eddie could just walk away from such an amazing relationship.

Finally, Audrey met a handsome, charismatic man named Colin. He was going through a rough breakup from a three-year dysfunctional relationship, yet he was so upbeat and positive. They had instant chemistry. Audrey could relate to how he was feeling, and he couldn't believe his good fortune. The first morning they woke up together, Colin said, "Wow, it feels so good to be happy again." Audrey completely identified. They became inseparable. Colin was making her feel desired again. She felt alive, wanted, and understood. After only a few days, Colin started to say to her, "You are everything I have ever wanted." She felt she could talk to him about anything. Colin promised her everything Eddie had failed to deliver, including having a baby. Audrey was a bit gun-shy and said, "Don't promise me that unless you know without a doubt that you can actually do it." "I've done that before," Colin reassured her. "I know exactly what I'm talking about. I loved being married; I just married the wrong person." He had gotten married in his early twenties and stayed married for more than ten years. He and his ex-wife had two children together but had divorced eight years before Audrey met him. Audrey had long believed Eddie's problem was that he had never really been in love before. He didn't know he had issues that would prevent him from keeping his promises. Colin understood heartbreak and personal loss. Audrey chose to trust him.

They had met through common friends, and about ten days later, while they were all out drinking, Colin asked in front of everyone, "Will you marry me?" Audrey was stunned but really happy. She answered, "I'm not saying no, but let's get to know each other a little more first." Colin agreed. But they were moving at a lightning-fast pace. Audrey met his family, Colin met hers, and they started to make plans to move in together. It was too fast for Audrey, but everyone in her life loved him, and he was offering her everything that she had always wanted. Most importantly, she was beginning to forget about Eddie. Colin was showing her that she could fall in love again, and she liked it. She started to go along with it all.

Colin's life was a mess from his previous relationship. Audrey took pleasure in helping him put the pieces back together. She helped him get a better apartment and was happily helping to decorate their new home. Everything seemed pretty comfortable for the first three months. Then one morning when they awoke, Colin seemed distant. Audrey knew something was wrong, but he wouldn't say what it was. She had a bad feeling in the pit of her stomach all day. She came home to find him sitting with a half-finished bottle of wine. "We need to talk," he said. "I can't have another baby." It wasn't just that; he was also wavering on the whole relationship. Audrey had just rearranged her whole life to move in with him. She couldn't believe it was happening again. "You promised," she said. "Well, I changed my mind," he coldly replied.

Audrey couldn't move out right away, and for the next few weeks, Colin kept flip-flopping his feelings. He'd be very unkind and distant, and then he would turn around and say, "I have never stopped loving you. I want to make this work. I'm just so confused." He started talking about his dysfunctional ex-girlfriend, who had been harassing him when Audrey first met him. All of a sudden it was clear to Audrey that she was Colin's rebound. Colin could clearly articulate why his previous relationship had been a nightmare for him. He had repeatedly told Audrey how much happier he was with her. He knew he didn't want his ex back, but he had never processed his hurt feelings from their breakup. He covered them up by falling in love with Audrey. It was an emotional mess. Audrey had to just walk away.

This story is a classic example of a between-meal snack. Colin was starving when he met Audrey. He couldn't get enough of her. But he wasn't ready for her. Timing is very important in a relationship. If a person were actually starving, you wouldn't begin to renourish them with a four-course well-balanced meal. You would start slowly and only give them what their body could handle, as they would need to become healthy before they could eat normally. Exactly the same principle applies to a person who is recovering from a painful breakup.

For Colin, it had only been two months since the end of an intense three-year relationship. Audrey truly was everything he had ever wanted. However, it was highly inappropriate for him to ask her to marry him before he truly knew her. He got caught up in the emotion of meeting someone who was actually good for him. Since he had fresh breakup wounds himself, he could identify with Audrey's heartache, and he wanted to make it better for her. She was making things better for him. He wasn't a bad guy, and he didn't intentionally or maliciously deceive her. He just didn't act responsibly. He couldn't digest all that she had to offer. He became overwhelmed, so he started to find fault with her to give himself some space. He pushed her away.

The bigger problem was that Colin had deep wounds that had nothing to do with any romantic relationships. His parents divorced when he was young, and his mother was tragically killed in an accident. He had also been in a couple car accidents; one scarred his face, and the other caused a death that scarred his heart. He was hurting and had deep abandonment issues. What he wanted with all his heart was a truly intimate loving relationship. He didn't want to be alone. But he had never taken the time to properly heal his issues. He kept distracting himself with inappropriate or dysfunctional relationships. When he met Audrey, there was no dysfunction to cover his real pain, so he started to feel it. All of his repressed emotion started to come to the surface. That is frequently the case. When you finally achieve what you most desire, that need is satisfied and you can stop chasing it. That makes room for other issues to get attention.

What really happened that day Audrey came home to Colin drinking by himself was that Colin had an emotional breakdown. He sobbed openly about the accidents and his past. Audrey tried to help him. He appreciated her support, but he wasn't ready to face those dark issues. He created dysfunction to push them back down again. Since Colin has abandonment issues and is not good at being alone, as soon as Audrey was completely gone, he immediately started dating someone new. Junk-food is currently more comfortable for Colin, at least subconsciously. He will keep running away from his issues until he is truly ready to confront and heal them. Only he can decide when that will be, if ever.

The good news for Audrey was that she moved on quickly too. She had been much further along in healing her personal issues and in processing her breakup with Eddie. Colin wasn't a good choice for her, but he did get into her heart, which helped her take down the wall she had been keeping around it since losing Eddie. That was a really good thing; regrettably, Colin hurt her again in the process. However, Colin was a lot easier to get over than Eddie. Audrey is now truly ready for a well-balanced meal.

If Colin had acted responsibly with his unstable feelings, they could have both simply enjoyed a hot fling to help them move forward. When you are going through a breakup and you're craving a between-meal snack, give yourself some rules to play by so no one—including you—gets hurt.

Rules for Consuming Between-Meal Snacks

1. Be honest with yourself. After a breakup, your feelings are usually confused. Be honest with yourself about what your situation truly is. Decide if the person you decide to be with is a good choice for you or just good temporarily to get you through your pain.

Check one:

____ This person is good for me.

____ I'm ignoring the junk-food flags because it's better to be with anyone than to be alone.

Check all that apply:

____ I have a habit of running from one relationship to the next.

____ I went out of my way to find a new relationship to ease the pain of my breakup.

____ This new relationship began spontaneously because this person was too good to pass up.

2. Be honest with your snack. Do you just want to have fun? Or are you genuinely looking to settle down in a real, emotionally intimate relationship? People get hurt when they have different perceptions about a common situation. If your between-meal snack is looking for a long-term relationship and you know he or she is just filling a need for you right now, you have to be honest. Be honest that you just got out of a significant relationship and that you can't offer anything more than a good time. I hate to say it, but chances are your snack won't hear you and will stay anyway, even if he or she does want more. At least in this case you will have been honest and cannot be blamed for being deceptive.

However, if you do genuinely feel like you are falling in love with your snack, do not tell him or her! You can say "You make me happy," "I enjoy being together," or "I'm glad we met," but what you are feeling may just be displaced feelings from your recent breakup. True love takes time to develop. If you do think you're falling in love, what's the hurry? Save using those powerful words until you have been together long enough to have your ex completely out of your mind. You shouldn't say "I love you" to someone until you are genuinely the only two in the relationship.

3. Give your snack a chance to become a well-balanced meal. If you just got out of a bad relationship that damaged your self-esteem, your snack may be showing you what a healthy meal is. The contrast may accelerate your feelings. It may also then burn them out. Timing has a lot to do with forming a true connection. If you think your snack is good for you but your feelings are starting to change, push the pause button. Someone healthy after junk-food may taste bland and boring. If this is the case, it is likely that your insecurity is growing. Deep inside you probably don't feel like you deserve someone healthy. But you do! You may also have become too dependent on your snack and it is scaring you. If the only nurturing you're getting is from the relationship, that's why you feel uncomfortable. You have to put your attention on taking care of yourself. Don't blame your snack if your feelings start to change; look inside and see what is going on with you. After you truly assess the situation, you can make a healthy decision about your future.

Playing Rules if You Are a Between-Meal Snack

1. Protect your heart. If you are the first person to start dating someone who has recently ended a significant relationship, be aware that your relationship will probably be short-lived. "Recent" means within a few months, or up to a year if it was a marriage or long-term relationship. Be very aware that the other person's feelings are unstable. She will be convinced that she loves you. You should be convinced that she is just feeling rescued. Enjoy her, but don't believe any of her feelings are real— at least not yet.

2. Take it slow. If he starts making plans for a future together, don't engage or agree with anything until you've been together at least six months. He may seem like he's making all your dreams come true. It is not real if you haven't known each other for at least six months! If you agree with any of the proposed plans, his feelings will most likely change.

3. Don't literally rescue them. If she just came out of a bad situation and her life is a mess, that should be a major junk-food flag and you should run in the other direction. If you really like her and choose to stay, you cannot become her caretaker. It's not your job to fix her life. You can be supportive. But do not lend her money or sacrifice any of your own needs to help her. She's supposed to be an adult. She'll ultimately have more respect for you if you let her solve her own problems. Keep your focus on taking care of you.

Doggie Bag
Stop Playing With Your Food

➡ **Don't play hard-to-get if you want a well-balanced meal.** Healthy communication is how real intimacy begins.

➡ **Don't create tests to judge the value of your relationship.** Keep your thoughts on you and what you think and feel. Don't decide you know what your partner is thinking and feeling. Allow him or her to show you.

➡ **Never flirt with another person to make your meal jealous.** Emotional intimacy cannot be achieved without trust and feeling safe with being vulnerable to your partner. Flirting with another destroys any opportunity for real intimacy, and therefore real love.

➡ **Don't get played by a player.** If your partner is not meeting all of your needs, don't make excuses for his or her bad behavior.

➡ **You can enjoy a between-meal snack if you stay true to yourself and your lover.** Don't make promises until you have known a person at least six months and until you know for sure that you can keep those promises.

Bruce Logan

CHAPTER FIVE

Forbidden Fruit

Forbidden fruit is anyone who is committed to someone else—emotionally, financially, or legally. That kind of unavailability can be very appealing to some people and, therefore, it is often consciously chosen with reckless disregard. Then again, forbidden fruit can also be bitten inadvertently while cleverly disguised as a healthy meal. No matter how it comes to be consumed, forbidden fruit will always produce heartburn that could have been avoided. This chapter is about taking care of yourself when you've fallen under the enchanting spell of forbidden fruit.

The Poisoned Apple

They say you should never judge a man until you've walked a mile in his shoes. But when it comes to dating a married man, people have some very strong opinions, whether they've ever walked in those shoes or not.

I have to acknowledge that, as a dating coach, my advice is to never date a married man or woman. I also know it's not always that black-and-white. Many times a woman has no idea the man she's dating is married. As a single woman, do you ask every date you have if he's married? Probably not, but it wouldn't necessarily make a difference if you did. Most married men who cheat don't wear a wedding ring and aren't straightforward about being married. Just like the poisoned apple, from the outside they look good enough to eat. Many unsuspecting women innocently fall for their deceptive charms. Then, when the truth is eventually revealed, the intense heartburn causes many smart women to make stupid choices. The pain of feeling betrayed can be all-consuming. The source of your comfort suddenly becomes the source of your pain. It's not easy to walk away, even when you know you should. This is especially true if he's trying to keep you by promising you the world and insisting there were extenuating circumstances. You may find yourself walking in shoes that you could have never even imagined would fit you.

You need to learn the signs to look for to identify a married man before you allow yourself to fall in love with him.

Note for men: Some married woman cheat too, but it has been my experience that they are usually upfront about it. However, simply change the pronoun if you suspect your woman may be married.

1. He's secretive with his phone. Nowadays many people don't have a home phone. So it's no big deal if you only have his cell number. How he uses the phone however, can be your best indicator of his availability.

- When you call him, does it always go to voicemail, and then he either calls you right back or only texts? He can listen to his voicemail and text in front of his wife, but he has to go somewhere else to take or place a call.

- Maybe you don't even have his number; does he always call from a blocked phone?

- Does he only text and never call?

- Does he take some phone calls in front of you but then step away from you to take others?

If he is secretive with his phone, that is probably an indicator that he's hiding something. Look for some of these other signs and consider him forbidden fruit if he does two or three more.

2. He only pays with cash. If he pays with cash, there is no record of where he is spending money. Using a credit or debit card could allow his wife to see the charges if she keeps the records or takes care of paying bills.

3. His time is very limited. A married man has someone else to be accountable to.

- Does he always seem to have a curfew, only meeting you for happy hour or for early dinners?

- Do you have a lot of daytime rendezvous that end with him going back to work?

- Does he disappear on weekends and only see you during the week?

All his communication might be confined to certain hours. Texting or calling in the middle of the night—while his wife is sleeping—might be the only private time he can get.

4. You don't know where he lives or have never been to his place. A married man usually can't bring you to his place, so he will always come to yours.

- He may give you some excuse for why he can't spend the whole night with you, such as he's a light sleeper or doesn't sleep well at other people's houses.

- He will be vague about where he lives because he can't have you dropping by unexpectedly.

- When you go out in public, it will always be somewhere close to your place. He won't want to run into anyone he knows near his home.

5. You only meet a few friends or none at all. A married man might have a small circle of friends who know he's unfaithful and don't disapprove. They're possibly unfaithful to their wives too. He could feel comfortable introducing you to them, but not to anyone in his family. It's easiest for him if you never meet anyone from his life at all. A single man who is crazy about you will want to show you off to all his friends and family.

6. He travels a lot for business. Not all people who travel for their work are cheaters. But it is worth noting that a man who travels for work can spend the night out of his home without creating suspicion. He can also tell you he's out of town when he is just home with his family.

7. If you met him online. Unfortunately, many married men who are looking to cheat find the Internet the best place to prey. It is a huge forbidden-fruit flag if he doesn't post a picture. A married man won't risk any of his wife's single friends seeing him on a dating website. His profile will be short but will make him sound like prince charming. He will try to rush you into bed. Take it slow. Also, some married men just like the fun and interaction of being online, with no intent to actually meet anyone. If you're communicating with a man who isn't asking to get together, move on to someone more available.

Some single men don't like to post a picture because of their business. Ask him his last name and where he works. Take extra caution with anyone who is vague or whom you can't find in a Google search.

Cut to the Core

If you suspect your man is married, you have to calmly ask him in person. Body language can be very revealing. People who are being untruthful tend to hesitate and blink a lot; some cover their mouth or touch their nose. He may even look away. Another sign of lying is using the question in the answer, or deflecting with another question. If you ask, "Are you married?" A normal response would simply be "No." But if he is married, he may answer, "Am I married? Why would you think that?" Or if he says "I am not married," it's more deliberate and most likely deceptive this way than if a contraction were used. A response more likely to be truthful would be "I'm not married."

A client I'll call Colleen met a man named Keith in a club. He was there with a group of people, but he was heavily flirting with her. She liked him and started to flirt back. He asked her to go to another club with him. Colleen and her girlfriend agreed. But before they left, a girl from Keith's group who had been acting jealous told Colleen that Keith was married. When they got to the next place, Colleen asked Keith. He replied, "Why are you with me if you think I'm married?" She said, "Well, your friend told me you are." He said, "I just met that girl tonight; she's not my friend." So Colleen let it go. She decided the girl was trying to "cock block" her and began dating Keith. However, he had never really answered her question. On a later date he told her he had never been married nor had kids and that he really wanted to finally do that. He even said he thought she might be *the one*. When they were together, it was amazing; he was attentive and expressive. But something never quite felt right; she just couldn't put her finger on what it was. When they weren't together, they were frequently fighting, mostly about not being together. Colleen was working very hard to make it work, and they hadn't even slept together yet—even though she really wanted to. I kept saying to her, "It's supposed to be easy. If it's like this in the beginning, where is it heading?" She couldn't get him out of her head. She believed they had something special. After several very frustrating months of his sporadic availability, she finally learned through an extensive Google search that he had a wife and son in another city. We had checked off five of the signs listed above in our talks; she just didn't want to acknowledge it.

Actions speak louder than words. Relationships are supposed to be easy in the beginning. That's when you're supposed to just be happy and enjoy each other. If that's not what you're experiencing, it's junk-food. Trust your instincts. Your gut will usually know when something isn't right—don't make excuses to try to reason it away. If your man is telling you he's not married but his behaviors include items from the list above, do some investigating. If he tells you he's separated but still living in the same house for financial reasons, that should be a deal-breaker. If he is not living in his own place for any reason, consider him forbidden fruit and move on. Unless he can show you legally filed separation papers, he is still married! He is not amazing if he is not fully available. Put yourself first.

Caught with Your Hand in the Cookie Jar

Probably the worst way to find out your amazing boyfriend has been lying to you is to be confronted by his wife. A client I'll call Morgan was in love with a wonderful man named Bill. They had been in a long-distance relationship for nine months. Bill had told Morgan he was married, but he had also said they were separated. His wife, Julia, was currently living in another city. Morgan had even spent the night at Bill's house, so she felt comfortable to believe him. He spoke openly about why his marriage had failed. It was largely because they stopped having sex when Julia learned she couldn't have a baby—she desperately wanted to become a mom. It tore them apart. Morgan felt compassion for Bill and was thrilled to give him the passionate sex life he had been craving. It was the most emotionally intimate relationship she had ever had. She felt that he knew what she needed even before she did. Morgan had never felt more loved. She wanted Bill to get a divorce so they could be married. He said financially he couldn't afford it yet and asked her to be patient. She was trying to be supportive.

During most of their relationship, Bill had been coming to New York to stay with Morgan. But things began to change when Morgan needed to come back to Chicago for work. Bill wanted her to come, but he wouldn't allow Morgan to stay with him. He confessed Julia was now back living with him for financial reasons—in a separate room, of course. Morgan didn't like it. They started to fight.

While in Chicago one night, Morgan came to pick Bill up at his house, as she had done several times before. Julia was in the driveway, putting some things in her trunk. Under the assumption that Julia knew Bill had a girlfriend (as Bill had told her), Morgan got out of the car to go to the door. That's what Julia had been waiting for. "Look," she said as she stopped Morgan, "I'm sure you're a nice girl. But Bill is my husband, not your boyfriend. Please leave him alone." Morgan was stunned. Her mouth was cotton dry as she replied, "Actually, he is my boyfriend. He told me that you're separated and that you knew he was seeing somebody." "We've never been separated," Julia replied. "We're trying to adopt a child."

Julia and Morgan sat down to talk—to compare notes, mostly. Bill had been living a double life. When Morgan had met Bill, Julia was temporarily staying in another city for her job. Bill was originally from New York, so Julia thought he had been going home to see his sick Mother. Julia couldn't stop crying. Morgan couldn't cry a single tear. She was in shock. Everything she thought she knew was a lie. Julia was beautiful, and she and Bill had a very active sex life. "We took a candlelit bath just last night," Julia said. That hurt. Morgan knew Bill loved baths, and she had had sex with Bill that afternoon. "Everyone tells me I have the most amazing husband," Julia said through her tears. "I know," Morgan said. "Everyone tells me I have the most amazing boyfriend."

Julia asked Morgan to please let him go. Morgan had to agree, but she was devastated.

If this should happen to you, be honest and try to take the high road. Whatever heartburn you are feeling, his wife is feeling worse. She did nothing wrong—he did. Tell her you didn't know. Give her any information she wants that might make her feel better, such as how he pursued you and how often you saw him. Do not feel like you need to give her identifying information like where you live or work. You don't want to make yourself vulnerable to any possible retaliation. To that point, it's better if you can avoid arguing with her. Again, your issue isn't with her; it's with him. He is not yours. While you have the opportunity, ask his wife anything that you want to know. If you've had suspicions, getting them clarified may help you let go.

In the above story, Julia was calm and rational when she approached Morgan. If this should happen to you and his wife is angry and lashing out, do not engage with her. Fighting with her could be dangerous, and it won't help either of you. If you can, ask if you can call her after she has had a chance to calm down. Let her know you will be happy to tell her your side of the story, but only if she can be calm.

If you have found out that your boyfriend is married and you're thinking about telling his wife, please think again. If you think that will cause her to leave him, odds are against you. As many as 87 percent of married couples stay together after an affair is revealed (I found statistics varying from 69 to 87 percent). Only 5 percent of relationships that begin as an affair survive.[22] It truly isn't worth it to go through all that drama and dysfunction for such a slim chance at winning a lying cheater. No matter how wonderful he may seem, he's not worth the heartburn. Put yourself first and walk away. You deserve better! Plus it's really not your place to intentionally intervene in his marriage.

Drinking the Juice

Jennifer called me hoping I could help her get her married boyfriend to finally leave his wife.

---

[22]"Dating a Married Man," Dr. Phil.com, December 9, 2012, http://www.drphil.com/articles/article/41.

He had been stringing her along for several years. She went on and on for more than two hours about him and why he was so great. Every time I tried to focus her attention on her and what was truly best for her, she brought the conversation back to him. She was convinced that he was best for her. I knew he wasn't, no matter how wonderful he seemed, because he wasn't truly hers. The more I tried to help her, the more she tried to manipulate me to get what she wanted. When I attempted to be firm and said, "I don't want to hear any more about him," she replied, "Now I want to cry; I need to tell you the whole story." So I let her continue. I didn't need to hear any more. She wasn't telling me anything that made me feel like he wanted to leave his wife. In fact, the more she said, the more I was sure he was never going to be exclusively hers. At the end of the session, Jennifer asked me if I thought I could help her. I answered by saying, "I don't think you'll allow me to help you." She cracked up and said, "Oh my God, you're probably right!" She didn't want to help herself. She just wanted her married man. I never heard from her again. If you are currently dating a married man or woman, I hope you'll choose to be wiser than Jennifer. I hope you will put yourself first and truly hear what I'm about to say.

> "The man who marries his mistress leaves a vacancy in that position."
> —Oscar Wilde

If he will cheat with you, he will cheat on you. He's junk-food! Your happiness has nothing to do with who he is; it's about you and what is best for you. Someone who is not completely available—for whatever reason—is bad for you and should be considered forbidden fruit.

It is estimated that only 5 percent of married men actually leave their wives for their mistress. I think that is because men don't cheat for the same reason women do. A woman usually cheats to find emotional fulfillment, to fill a void in her marriage. A man usually cheats to create excitement, and even danger, in his ordinary life. A man doesn't have to be unhappy in his marriage to cheat; he can just be susceptible to temptation. Of course, if he told a potential mistress he just wanted to use her for his own pleasure, she probably wouldn't be interested. So he spins a web of lies. He tells her what he thinks she needs to hear: that he's emotionally unfulfilled, that he's sexually neglected, and that he and his wife have grown apart. No matter what he is telling her, his marriage is fulfilling him in some way; otherwise, he would have already left on his own. People do what they want to do. He wants to be with his wife; he just wants his mistress too. If you are dating a married man I know this is hard to hear, but he is absolutely still having sex with his wife, and he is enjoying it! If you are saying to yourself that your man is different, you're kidding yourself. He's just a really good liar.

The beginning of an affair is exciting and romantic. It's a bit of a game to find stolen moments and passionate getaways. Lunchtime sex feels mischievous and caring. But as time passes and that new relationship euphoria wears off, you will start seeing less and less of your man. You start to become part of his schedule, and it becomes more of a routine then a thrilling adventure. He may genuinely develop feelings for you, but do not kid yourself into believing that those feelings mean he has lost his deep affinity for his wife. He took vows with her; they sleep in the same bed every night. They share a connection that you don't have with him. You have a function in his life that he probably does truly enjoy, but he likes it just the way it is and he doesn't want to change it. If it did change and you were his full-time love, he probably wouldn't want you anymore. Statistics show that less than 5 percent of relationships that start as an affair survive. If you are choosing to carry on a relationship with a married man, be prepared to accept the situation as it is. Do not expect him to leave his wife.

If you're saying that you don't need him to leave his wife and that you're just happy to be his mistress, then I have to say that you should be careful what you wish for. That is a very unfulfilling life. You deserve better.

Symptoms of consuming forbidden fruit

1. Your needs will never come first. He has to put his spouse and family first. He will squeeze in your needs only when it's convenient for him. You will always come second, or even third.

2. You are a dirty little secret. Some of your select friends may know, but you can never meet his parents, siblings, or family friends. If he has kids, you will never know them. You will always be kept in the shadow of his first life.

3. You will spend holidays alone. You had better have a full, active life of your own. You will never have a full life with him.

4. You are playing the waiting game. You're waiting for him to call because you can't openly call him. You're waiting to steal some alone time with him. Let's face it; you're waiting for him to leave his wife. He won't—at least not for you.

A man or woman who truly loved you would never subject you to the above treatment. If you truly loved yourself, *you* wouldn't put up with it.

Pick Your Poison

I do understand the magnetic pull toward someone you think is the love of your life. I also understand if you feel you will never find that kind of chemistry with anyone else ever again. But I assure you that going after or giving in to a lover who is committed to someone else is a recipe for inevitable heartburn. I believe there are two possible reasons you are willing to subject yourself to forbidden fruit.

1. Low self-esteem

A person with healthy, high self-esteem will never settle for a person who is committed to someone else in any way. Review chapter one, "Heartburn," page 40, and really be honest with yourself about what you want. Do some soul-searching on what is truly best for you. I hope this book is giving you healthy food for thought.

2. Commitmentphobia

Chapter two, "Binging and Purging," page 62, taught you that a person with commitment issues will always choose an unavailable person, whether consciously or subconsciously. The most definite form of unavailability is to be committed to someone else. Real emotional intimacy can never be achieved in a triangle relationship. If you are choosing to be involved with a man or woman who is married, I hope you will consider the possibility that you have commitment issues.

Doggie Bag
Forbidden Fruit

➡ **Trust your instincts.** Actions speak louder than words. If your partner acts unavailable, he or she is unavailable.

➡ **Value yourself.** Enforce healthy boundaries and know you deserve someone who wants to commit exclusively to you. Never choose to accept being second.

➡ **Protect your heart.** If you believe forbidden fruit could be the love of your life, do not have sex with that person until he or she is legally separated and living in a separate house.

➡ **If you get caught by your partner's spouse,** take the high road and be honest. You are the outsider and do not have a commitment with this forbidden fruit.

➡ **Don't carelessly destroy relationships.** If the person you desire is committed to someone you know, or are related to, know without a doubt that being with such a person will destroy a friendship or family bond. Make sure this man or woman will stay with you till death do you part and is truly worth it. Otherwise, he or she is forbidden fruit.

CHAPTER SIX

Food Poisoning

We've all probably known someone (or perhaps this is you) who was happy and pleasant to be friends with until he or she became crazy about some girl or guy, and then he or she completely changed. And I don't mean that in a positive way. A person who goes from being a pleasure to be around—to someone whom you avoid even taking a phone call from. All they do is complain, and no matter what great advice you may give them they keep going back for more dysfunction or abuse. They're with a vampire—the kind of person that sucks the energy out of people. Do you know the type? This sort of relationship makes people insecure, obsessive, defensive, and certainly not happy—all symptoms of consuming junk-food. And when it starts to make them physically ill, their partner is food poisoning.

Have you ever had food poisoning? I have. It's awful! One time I got sick after eating a salad in a restaurant. A salad! Who would think a salad would make you sick? After three days of nonstop violent illness, I managed to drag myself to see my doctor. He suggested perhaps they had cut the salad with the same knife they had used to cut raw meat. Whatever it was, I didn't see it coming. The second time, I got it from eating leftover pasta salad that had not been refrigerated for several hours. In hindsight, I should have known not to eat it, but I was hungry and it was the only thing there. So I ate it—big mistake.

Relationships can be toxic just like some food. Sometimes it is hard to see it coming. Most of the time there is a warning sign to alert you of the danger, if you choose to heed it. Many people consider an abusive relationship to mean involvement with a physically violent man or woman who hits and leaves marks. While that is accurate, it is not the only way a relationship can be abusive. Abuse can also be verbal, emotional, sexual, financial, and even neglectful.

> It's not only men who can be abusive.
>
> Women are frequently abusive too.

There is usually a lot of "love" along with the abuse, which can make the relationship feel very confusing. Just like *actual* food poisoning, you'll know you have it when you start to feel ill. Be honest with yourself. Have you changed into someone you don't really like or perhaps don't even recognize anymore? That can be your best indicator of someone who is toxic to you.

Love as a Drug

Finding a love connection is intoxicating. To deeply and passionately connect with another human being can be the holy grail of life. To find your *soul mate* is a dream come true. So when you first start to fight, you usually just let it go—because you found your *one*. Then the next time the fight is a little bit worse; you cry, and it's kind of out of control. But the next day she apologizes. She accepts all the blame, saying that she knows she was wrong. She tells you how wonderful you are and promises she won't do it again. You happily forgive her and move on—until it happens again, and then again. Each time, it gets worse. Most toxic relationships have high intensity. They exist on a cycle of tremendous highs, dysfunctional lows and despair, and passionate makeups. All the while you keep holding on to the hope of the amazing love you initially shared, and there are still glimpses of it that keep you staying for more.

> One of the hardest things to learn is that loving someone with all of your heart is not a good enough reason to stay with him or her. You have to love yourself most.

Shelly fell in love with a funny, creative, sensitive, and intelligent man named Adam. They stayed up all night talking about things she had never talked about with anyone. They were in the same business, and she was learning a lot from him. He understood her in a way that no one else ever had. For the first time in her life, she understood what a soul mate was. She had found her *one.* So the first time Adam said something really mean to her, she was stunned. All she could do was cry. He melted. He couldn't apologize enough. He said, "Please don't cry. I can't stand that I made you cry. I love you so much." They made love and everything was back to normal—until the next time. Adam started to yell at her a lot. Shelly is a sweet, beautiful girl, and Adam was terrified of losing her. He was threatened by other men who found her attractive. He blamed Shelly if she didn't act exactly as he wanted. Shelly tried to defend herself, but that just made their arguments more intense. During one of their fights, Shelly cried, and this time Adam said, "Oh boo-hoo, shut up!" Shelly couldn't believe who he had turned into. But she stayed because the next day he told her he didn't want to lose her and that she was the best thing that had ever happened to him. He said, "You're so good to me. I know I don't deserve you." Shelly just wanted to love him more. He was going through a hard time financially; she assumed that was making him irritable. She wanted to help him.

Shelly had met Adam through common friends who entertained a lot. Adam started picking fights on the way to their house, even keeping it going as they got out of their car. Then he would immediately drop it the second their friends answered the front door. He'd walk in as if nothing had happened, but Shelly would be choking back tears. She'd try to smile but couldn't say a word. She knew that if she opened her mouth, she'd break down. It made her appear moody and withdrawn. People would ask Adam, "What's wrong with her?" He'd pretend he didn't know.

Throughout the evening he'd take shots at her to get laughs. At first she would just shyly take it. But eventually she started to fight back.

Shelly tried to keep a life outside of Adam's world. Every time she went out with her friends, he would blow-up her phone (call her repeatedly) and cause problems. He'd accuse her of cheating and try to catch her in lies. Shelly was being honest. She just wanted some time without him. Her friends would constantly tell her to leave him. "Why do you put up with that?" they would ask. She didn't think she did; she always stood up for herself and kept her own apartment. She didn't recognize that staying with him *was* putting up with it. Being with Adam was diminishing her self-esteem. Her energy was negative; it was spilling over into other areas of her life. Her career was suffering, and her relationships with others changed. Everyone kept telling her that her life would be better without Adam. She couldn't see that. She thought she needed him. After a while she stopped doing things that she wanted to do; it just wasn't worth the argument with Adam.

Adam was a heavy drinker, and Shelly had learned to enjoy fine wine. She could stop at two glasses. Adam would drink until he passed out. He used to say, "At least I'm a happy drunk." But in reality he was an angry drunk. Alcohol and anger are a bad combination. Shelly found herself engaging in the arguments. Adam pushed her to a rage that she didn't recognize in herself. It scared her, but she couldn't walk away. She was frustrated. He was still her best friend, but he could turn on her for what seemed like no reason. Soon it wasn't just verbal sparring. Adam never hit her, but they had some knock-down, drag-out fights. He'd wrestle her to the ground and shove her out the door, and he damaged some expensive things. One night when Shelly was driving Adam's car home, Adam was drunk and didn't like the way she was driving. He punched his windshield three times, leaving shatter marks each place his fist connected. Shelly drove him home in silence. Then she got in her car and went to her apartment. The next morning, Adam wanted to take her to breakfast to apologize. When Shelly got there, he made her take his car to get the windshield fixed. He was too embarrassed.

Shelly broke up with Adam many times. He'd always do something really sweet to get her back. He'd buy her a nice gift or take her on a romantic vacation. There would always be a "second honeymoon" stage. When it was good, it was great. But when it was bad, it was abusive. This went on for more than four years. Shelly loved Adam. She knew Adam loved her. But she didn't feel loved. She felt manipulated and controlled.

The friend who introduced them was Adam's best friend. He finally said to her, "I love Adam too. But he's not good for you. You need to get away from him." Shelly was trying.

It came to the point at which they were fighting on a daily basis. Their sexual connection had always been strong, so Shelly told Adam that she wouldn't have sex with him again until five days had passed without him arguing with her. He agreed. But then he couldn't do it. Every time he yelled at her or said something mean, Shelly would say, "It's back to day one." Adam would say, "No, I didn't mean that. I take it back." He was trying so hard to be good. It finally started to sink in for Shelly that Adam just wasn't capable of being nice to her.

Finally, Shelly learned not to engage with Adam, but to just walk away. If they were driving in the car, she would just look out the window and not respond to anything negative he said. Initially it would make him yell more, but he couldn't argue with himself, and eventually he would just stop. They started taking two cars everywhere they went so Shelly could leave anytime she wanted. Just because they went somewhere together didn't mean they would come home together. Then one night, when they were drinking heavily at Adam's house, Adam started to verbally abuse Shelly. She didn't want to drive, so she just went to bed. He wanted her to stay up with him. He jumped on top of her and started yelling. She wouldn't respond. In his frustration, he held a pillow over her face. She couldn't breathe. She started to fight back, but it just made Adam more aggressive. The pillow was so tight on Shelly's face she that couldn't even tell him she couldn't breathe. She stopped fighting and just lay still. He finally let go.

Shelly couldn't stop crying. She knew Adam could have killed her. She knew that wasn't his intention, but she would have been dead just the same. She started packing up all the things she had at his house. She had done this many times before. This time was different. This time his abuse had finally sunk in. Adam was following her around, trying to make light of it. "Stop being dramatic," he said, "I didn't hurt you." Shelly ignored him. As she put her things in her car, Adam said, "Why don't you just leave it; you know you're coming back." As she got in the car to leave, she turned and said, "Not this time Adam. I'm done." She finally was.

Shelly had never considered her relationship with Adam to be abusive. In many ways he protected her and helped her out. She knew it was dysfunctional, but she had grown up in a very dysfunctional home, so it seemed normal to her. Two years into their relationship, Adam had wanted them to get help. She was encouraged that he seemed open to change. She thought that if he could change his anger outbursts, they could be happy again. Unfortunately, he started an argument in the parking lot and left her there. Adam didn't think he needed help; he wanted to fix her. He wanted her to be more obedient. Shelly did engage with him and fight back. However, that just made her a participant, not the catalyst. Regardless, her resistance doesn't make any of Adam's actions Shelly's fault.

If any part of this story has you nodding your head and identifying elements of your own relationship, you are in an abusive relationship. This kind of behavior is not normal. It is unhealthy. You deserve better! It doesn't matter what you have done or who you are. There are men and women out there who would never behave like Adam. Love yourself first and trust that there is a better match for you—if you can find the strength to walk away from this one. If your abusive partner is the mother or father of your children, that is still no excuse to stay. You need to set a better example for your kids. You need to get them out of the abusive environment.

Mishandling Food

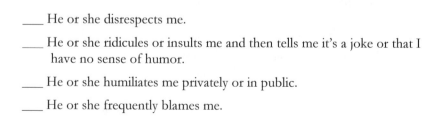

It's hard to admit that someone you love isn't good for you. Friends and family may try to tell you what they see, but until you are ready to hear who your mate truly is, you will keep doing what you want. Shelly wrote a list of pros and cons. Her biggest pro was that she loved him. But her cons list was two pages longer than her pros list. Use the list below as a guide for your cons list. Place a check mark on the line next to each behavior your partner has exhibited.

____ He or she disrespects me.

____ He or she ridicules or insults me and then tells me it's a joke or that I have no sense of humor.

____ He or she humiliates me privately or in public.

____ He or she frequently blames me.

____ He or she harasses me about imagined affairs.

____ He or she manipulates me with lies and contradictions.

____ He or she acts immature and selfish yet accuses me of those behaviors.

____ He or she ignores my feelings.

____ He or she rolls his or her eyes when I speak or have an opinion.

____ He or she ridicules my beliefs, religion, race, heritage, class, or gender.

____ He or she withholds his or her approval, appreciation, affection, or sex.

____ He or she gives me the silent treatment.

____ He or she walks away without answering me.

____ He or she has left me stranded.

____ He or she criticizes me, calls me names, and yells at me.

____ He or she repeatedly hassles me about things I did in the past.

____ He or she hassles me about socializing with my friends or family.

____ He or she constantly checks up on me, reads my e-mail, and calls my phone repeatedly.

____ He or she isolates me.

____ He or she tries to prevent me from doing things I want to do.

____ He or she makes me keep up appearances even when I don't feel well.

____ He or she gets angry if I pay too much attention to another person or thing.

____ He or she interferes with my work or school. (Starts an argument before I go or makes harassing calls while I'm there.)

____ He or she makes sure that I don't get what I want.

____ He or she tells me that I'm too sensitive.

____ He or she hurts me more when I'm feeling down.

____ He or she likes to argue.

____ He or she has unpredictable mood swings; things are fine and then go bad for no apparent reason.

____ He or she always puts on a pleasant face to the world and is well liked by   outsiders.

____ He or she twists my words, somehow turning what I say against me.

____ He or she tries to control my decisions, money, and even the way I look, style my hair, or wear my clothes.

____ He or she complains about how badly I treat him or her.

____ He or she threatens to leave me or to throw me out.

____ He or she prevents me from leaving.

____ He or she says things that make me feel good but then does things that make me feel bad.

____ He or she has threatened to hurt me or my family.

____ He or she has hit or pushed me, even *accidentally*.

____ He or she has threatened me with a knife, gun, or other weapon.

____ He or she destroys furniture, punches holes in walls, and breaks major items.

____ He or she throws things.

____ He or she apologizes and promises to never do something hurtful again.

____ He or she seems to stir up trouble just when we seem to be getting closer to each other.

____ He or she abuses something I love, such as a pet, a child, or my things.

____ He or she compliments me enough to keep me happy yet criticizes me enough to keep me insecure.

____ He or she questions my every move and motive, doubting my competence.

____ He or she interrupts me and never really listens.

____ He or she makes me feel like I can't win. I'm damned if I do, damned if I don't.

___ Things get worse when he or she uses drugs or alcohol.

___ He or she provokes me to rage and then uses that as proof it's all my fault.

___ He or she tries to convince me I'm always wrong.

___ He or she says things then later denies it or accuses me of misunderstanding.

___ He or she treats me like a sex object or as though I should provide sex on demand regardless of how I feel.

___ He or she pressures me to do sexual acts that hurt or that I don't like.

___ He calls me slut, whore, or bitch.

___ She calls me loser, or asshole.

___ He or she makes public sexual advances.

___ He or she makes comments about my sexual abilities in public.

___ He or she forces me to have sex with other people.

If you checked off more than five things in the above list you have food poisoning. It doesn't matter how much you love him or her. Love cannot outweigh any of the above cons. You cannot change them! He or she may end up killing you—even if they don't mean to. You have to get away from this toxic person! It is not your fault he or she treats you the way they do. I promise you, there is a better life waiting for you outside of this relationship. The first step toward finding it is letting go.

Love isn't supposed to hurt.

If you are living with your partner and he or she has physically hurt you, call the **National Domestic Violence Hotline at 1-800-799-SAFE**. It doesn't matter if he or she only hit you once or that he or she never meant to hurt you. Just call the number and tell them your story. They will tell you if you're truly in danger. They will help you. They offer help for abusers too. **http://www.thehotline.org**

If you are in any kind of abusive relationship, the National Domestic Violence Hotline can help you. Visit their website to learn about all they have to offer. If your partner hasn't physically hurt you but is verbally and emotionally abusive, they will still help you. If you live with him or her and can't afford to move out, there are housing resources available to you. If you don't feel comfortable to call the hotline, confide in a trusted friend or family member and see if you can stay with him or her for a while. If you don't have a family member to stay with, you can apply for public assistance. You are going to need a lot of loving support. Don't be embarrassed; it is not your fault. Abusive relationships badly damage self-esteem. People who love you will understand and want to help. Look for a support group in your area. It is helpful to meet other men and women going through the same thing. Make sure you are not alone. He will probably try to come back. He will make all the same apologies and promises, but he has not changed. Real change takes time and requires professional abuse counseling. Stay strong and believe you deserve better. It may be difficult to walk away from him, but your life will get so much better when he is out of your life.

If you checked off three to five things in the above list, then your meal is junk-food. Junk-food isn't healthy, and you need to let go and look for someone healthier.

Hangovers and Munchies

Having a positive attitude and being a supportive partner is something I highly recommend—unless you're dating an addict. When you first meet an alcoholic, you may not see his or her drinking as a problem. Drinking  is very social, and when you're attracted to someone it's easy to get swept up into the moment. Many relationships begin by talking and drinking all night and then falling into bed for hot, drunken sex. If you don't have a problem with alcohol, you probably won't see that as anything to worry about. In fact, you'll probably be excited you found a great connection. Alcoholics can be friendly, outgoing, and the life of the party—all coping skills they had to learn to cover up their deep shame and unhealed pain. When intoxicated, they can become an open book. It's easy to mistake that behavior as emotionally availability. Especially for women who are nurturing by nature, it seems natural to feel compassion for an emotional guy. Particularly if he's really hot. You get drawn in before you even have a chance to recognize what you're in for. What you really need to do is run in the other direction.

In the story of Shelly and Adam earlier in this chapter, Adam was an alcoholic. Most abusive relationships involve alcohol and/or drug use. If you are involved with an addict, you are actually in a triangle relationship. Your lover's first priority is his or her disease. Be it alcohol or hard drugs, he or she will lie, manipulate, cheat, steal, or do whatever it takes to get their next fix. If you try to intervene, they will lash out. When I say you can't change anyone, that is especially true of addicts. You may think that all your problems would go away if he or she would just stop drinking or taking drugs. Unfortunately, that is never the case.

Addicts become addicted because they can't stand themselves sober. Most of them grew up in a broken and/or dysfunctional home, usually with an angry and abusive alcoholic. As adults they act out the behavior modeled for them as a kid. They are usually in denial and think, or at least say, they could stop drinking or using anytime they wanted. They may even stop for a few days to try to prove their point, but they'll soon become irritable and return to drinking to take the edge off. If it ever comes down to a choice between you and an addict's addiction, their drug of choice will always win. For that very reason, you need to always put yourself first.

Abuse is abuse; addicts can exhibit the same behaviors you checked off in the previous section. If you are dating an addict, it is just a matter of time before he or she hurts you or becomes abusive. Your love cannot help them. Only the addict can decide if he or she is ready to get help, and even then it's a long and difficult process. Abuse frequently intensifies as he or she tries to get sober. Get out of the line of fire and save yourself.

The following checklist will help you recognize an addict before you get too involved. If you can check off three or more symptoms and behaviors below, he or she is food poisoning and will only make you ill if you stay.

____ All our dates involve heavy drinking.

____ He or she can drink a lot without seeming drunk.

____ He or she *always* has more than just one drink.

____ Everything he or she does involves drinking.

____ He or she doesn't go places that do not serve alcohol.

____ He or she has a drink before we go out.

____ He or she has alcohol in place of a meal.

____ Once he or she starts drinking, he or she drinks until falling asleep or passing out.

____ He or she gets defensive if I question his or her drinking.

____ He or she is moody and irritable when not drinking, but happy and enjoyable when drinking.

____ He or she neglects work, school, or other responsibilities to drink.

____ He or she is behind in his or her bills or rent but still buying alcohol and/or going out.

____ We miss or are late for appointments because of him or her.

____ When I'm with him or her, I drink more than I usually do.

____ I have ridden in the car with him or her after he or she has been drinking.

____ I've told a lie to cover up his or her drinking.

____ I have been hurt or embarrassed by his or her behavior.

If you're unconvinced you should leave a relationship with an addict, I highly recommend finding an Al-Anon meeting in your area. Al-Anon is for people who love an addict. Visit www.al-anon.org for more information.

Arsenic in Your Drinking Water

There is a specific kind of toxic relationship that is hard to initially recognize. If you are unfortunate enough to fall in love with a sociopath, you will most definitely begin to feel like there is arsenic in your drinking water— and he or she will make you feel like you're the crazy one. Arguably one of the most famous sociopaths is Charles Manson, who masterminded the brutal killings at

Sharon Tate's house. If you have ever seen video of him speaking, you would likely think it would be next to impossible to fall in love with a man like that. On the contrary, most sociopaths are incredibly charismatic. They are highly skilled at influencing others with their intellect, wit, and exaggerated stories. They frequently exude an irresistible sexuality. When you first meet a sociopath, it's undeniably difficult *not* to be taken by him or her.

You may already know a sociopath. The Mayo Clinic estimates that 3 to 5 percent of men and 1 percent of women are afflicted by antisocial personality disorder. Most of them are not psychotic killers and will never physically harm you. What does make them all dangerous is that their brains lack the ability to feel essential social emotions, such as empathy, remorse, shame, and guilt. They are incapable of forming emotional attachments. They are fascinated with society. They emotionally seduce people and use them for their own personal gain. If one sets his or her sights on you, he or she will most likely pull out all the stops and lay it on thick.

Needless to say, you can never achieve emotional intimacy with a sociopath. He has no conscience and no remorse and can't feel love. He can be very attentive and deceptive, and will pretend to be in love in order to get what he wants. If you fall for a sociopath's charms and allow yourself to be vulnerable, he will without a doubt destroy you—and take pleasure in it. Do not give him that opportunity. Here are some signs to help you identify a sociopath.

1. He or she is charismatic and charming. Of course, not all charismatic people are sociopaths. But be leery if he or she is a smooth talker and an elegant dresser with impeccable manners and a flair for seduction and romance. He or she will be very exciting and never miss a beat.

2. You have intense sexual chemistry. Both male and female sociopaths have elevated levels of testosterone. He or she may have an insatiable sexual appetite, or even weird or kinky fetishes. A female sociopath may give a man the most mind-blowing sex he has ever experienced. It's easy to become addicted to sex with a sociopath. Be careful, as that is what pulls most people in to their spell.

3. You can see it in his or her eyes. When he or she looks into your eyes, do you feel uncomfortable and get a chill? Not in the good way that makes your heart skip a beat, but the kind that runs down the back of your spine. Do you feel more like prey then a lover?

4. He or she tells outrageous stories. Sociopaths exaggerate wildly. They'll make up some unbelievable story but tell it in such a captivating way that you believe them. They may even be poetic. Sociopaths are master wordsmiths.

5. He or she has an enormous ego. He acts like the smartest, richest, and most successful man in the room. She acts like the most beautiful and expects special treatment. A sociopath will probably even tell you how amazing he or she is.

6. He or she is a blamer. Nothing is ever his or her fault. Sociopaths will always have an excuse for why things didn't go right. They can't feel guilt, so they will never apologize.

7. He or she is highly intelligent. Sociopaths tend to have high IQs. They are skilled at attracting a following. Unfortunately they use their brainpower to deceive, manipulate, and control people rather than to empower them.

8. He or she needs to win at all costs. Sociopaths hate to lose an argument. They will defend their web of lies so aggressively that they frequently become more and more absurd—and unbelievable.

9. He or she can't feel love. It may seem as though you're dating Dr. Jekyll and Mr. Hyde. One minute he or she loves you, and the next he or she could not care less about you—literally. He or she is incapable of feeling empathy or love. He or she doesn't care about you but will pretend to when it suits him or her.

10. He or she is spontaneous and erratic. Sociopaths do not conform to society, so they may take extreme risks or do other impulsive things that seem bizarre or unusual. He or she has no conscience and no fear of regret.

11. He or she creates chaos wherever he or she goes. Sociopaths present themselves as having high morals and effortlessly attract followers. Then they'll turn people against each other and refuse to see their role in creating the problem.

12. You can't reason with a sociopath. Sociopaths are delusional. They will make a statement and then take it as the gospel truth. You cannot change their mind. If you try to reason with a sociopath, they will debate you to the point of exhaustion. That is, if they don't just get angry and turn on you.

If you already know someone who you suspect may be a sociopath, you can take the following actions to uncover the truth.

1. Trust your instincts. If you meet someone who's incredibly charismatic and seems too good to be true—assume he or she is. Delay getting intimate and take your time getting to know him or her (this is always a good idea). He or she will try to rush you, and you'll start to get a feeling that something is not right. Trust your instincts! Don't make any excuses for anything he or she does. Don't allow him or her to manipulate you. Save yourself now. Just stop seeing this person.

2. Fact-check his or her stories. Sociopaths are wild exaggerators and masters of deception. They have no guilt or shame, so they spin an elaborate web of lies. They will be vague about specifics. Ask questions about the details of their life. Try to pin down where they went to school, when, with whom, etc. But you can't check their stories with people who know them, as those people may be under their hypnotic spell (metaphorically speaking). Google them and the information they give you to see what you can verify. It may even be worth it to spend the money for a background check. You can find out if they have ever been married or if they have a criminal record. Sociopaths are great con artists.

3. Carefully confront him or her with his or her lies. Only confront the person to confirm your suspicions, *not* to take any real action. Do not confront him or her by yourself. If you show a sociopath proof of a lie he or she told, the sociopath will look away and try to avoid it. If the sociopath cannot get away, he or she will get angry, threaten you, and attack you. A sociopath will never admit he or she is wrong. He or she will invent a new set of lies to explain away what you present to him or her.

If you are already in a relationship with a person who you suspect may be a sociopath, use the above methods to confirm what you fear. Get out now if you think there is even a chance he or she is a sociopath. Sociopaths cannot be rehabilitated or changed. Their brains are hardwired. For change to be possible, a sociopath would have to first admit there was something wrong with him. A sociopath cannot do that. Sometimes sociopaths are court ordered to get help, but because they are master manipulators and liars, the help does not work, as therapy cannot work without honesty and a sense of self-responsibility. Medications can cure some behaviors of sociopaths, but there is no medicine to teach them how to feel emotions. You cannot teach someone to feel love, fear, guilt, empathy, or remorse for his or her actions. If someone cannot feel those emotions, he or she cannot feel what is right and what is wrong. A sociopath is deadly food poisoning. He or she can do a lot of damage to your physical and mental health. Don't put any more effort into this relationship. Take care of yourself. Nurture yourself. Food poisoning takes some time to recover from. Most importantly, get far away from your sociopath. And stay away—no matter what.

Doggie Bag

Food Poisoning

➡ **Decide if your relationship is abusive.** The way you feel is your best indicator of abuse. Love is not supposed to hurt. If you do not *feel* loved and positively supported, your relationship is not good enough for you.

➡ **If you are in an abusive relationship, get out now!** Put yourself first. Tell friends and family members what is happening. It is not your fault! You *will* find a better relationship if you leave this one.

➡ **Don't isolate yourself.** Surround yourself with supportive friends and family. Find a support group.

➡ **Think for yourself.** Don't let anyone tell you that your opinions are wrong, invalid, or unimportant.

➡ **Trust your instincts.** If anything doesn't feel right, assume it's not. Don't rationalize away bad behavior.

➡ **Enforce healthy boundaries.** Fool me once, shame on you; fool me twice, shame on me. Once someone has showed you who he or she is, accept it. He or she will not change. The next chapter will help you learn how to enforce healthy boundaries.

➡ **Do not try to change an addict.** Addicts can only be helped if they want to change for themselves. Trying to help an addict who doesn't want help is like banging your head against a wall. Stop! You cannot control them. Put yourself first.

➡ **Nurture your self-esteem.** Abuse beats down your self-esteem. Use the exercise in chapter one, "Heartburn," on page 48.

CHAPTER SEVEN

Relationship Crash Diet

If you wanted to change your outward appearance, you could possibly cut and color your hair, buy new clothes, and change your makeup or grow facial hair. But the most dramatic physical makeovers usually involve going on some sort of a diet. Fasts and pills, all protein, no carbs—there are many different approaches, but the bottom line always comes down to calories out verses calories in: diet and exercise. No matter how you choose to achieve it, no one else can do it for you. *You* have to take action to burn off more than you consume.

If you want to change your relationships, the same principle applies. You need to be aware of what you're giving out and make healthy choices about what you take in. It's not about anyone else or what they do. As a dating and relationship coach, the question I am most often asked by singles is, "What are people looking for?" Well, to me that question incites a different question: "What are you looking for?" The answer is not really about what anyone else thinks of you. It's not about what he or she wants, likes, or does. It's all about you! It's about what you think, what you feel, and what you choose. It's about truly knowing how you are fabulous—everyone is—and not settling for anyone who isn't smart enough to recognize your fabulousness.

We're all mind readers in a sense, because energy is contagious. Whatever you're thinking or feeling about yourself on the inside will be the energy you project on the outside. You are what you think you are. Therefore, everyone else thinks that of you too. So if you're thinking, "She'd never be interested in me," that's why she's not. And if you're thinking, "I can't keep a man," that's why you can't.

Your thoughts create your feelings. Then your feelings cause you to act or react. Your actions produce your results. If you want a different result, it really is as simple as changing your thinking. Of course, I realize that is easier said than done. That's why I wrote this book.

Start by asking yourself what you're really looking for. Forget about what any guy or girl might want. In fact, forget about dating altogether for now. This is about *you*. Take a good, long look at yourself, beyond just the reflection you see in the mirror. Look into your heart and your mind. What do you see? Do you like who you are? Are you comfortable with you? What do you really want? None of these questions have anything to do with anyone else. But when you find happiness for yourself in the answers, you will be very attractive to others.

This chapter is intended to be a crash diet to help you improve your relationships. The exercises that follow will help you contemplate, take responsibility for, and improve your reality.

BECOME A FORTIFIED SUPERFOOD

How many times have you heard the expression "You're giving away your power"? It has become very mainstream. Do you really know what it means? Take the following quiz and circle the answer that best describes how you typically respond to situations.

Quiz: Are You Giving Away Your Power?

____ 1. After I give a hot girl or guy my phone number, or after I get a hot girl's or guy's phone number,

    A.) I ask when he is going to call, or when I should call.

    B.) I tell all my friends I met the person of my dreams.

    C.) I go on with my life as if nothing changed.

    D.) I clear my schedule so I'll be available to go out when he calls.

    E.) I call him if I don't hear from him right away.

____ 2. When I start dating a new meal,

    A.) I try to be everything she wants me to be.

    B.) I put on my best behavior until I know I have her.

    C.) I'm an open book. I tell her everything about me.

    D.) I take it slowly and keep watch for possible junk-food flags.

    E.) I get really excited and fantasize about the possibilities of our future together.

____ 3. When a girl or guy rejects or breaks up with me,

    A.) I think about him a lot and wonder why he didn't want me.

    B.) I send him an e-mail telling him how I feel.

    C.) I acknowledge that he is not right for me and focus on myself.

    D.) I spy on him to see who else he is with.

    E.) I keep calling him to try to get him back.

____ 4. If another girl or guy is flirting with my meal,

    A.) I get angry at my meal for encouraging him.

    B.) I get quiet and withdraw.

C.) I show off and one-up him to make sure my meal knows I'm better.

D.) I tell the guy off and/or act nasty toward him.

E.) I playfully tell my meal how desirable she is and how much I appreciate her.

____ 5. When I'm crazy about a girl or guy,

A.) I work really hard to make sure nothing goes wrong.

B.) I make him my top priority.

C.) I let him take the lead to make sure he is happy.

D.) It scares me. I don't want to get hurt, so I push him away.

E.) I want to spend all my free time with him.

____ 6. When my meal does something that upsets me,

A.) I do something that will upset my meal to show her how it feels.

B.) I cry so she will know to apologize.

C.) I ask her to talk about it so that it won't happen again.

D.) I withdraw and take it as a sign that she doesn't love me.

E.) I yell at my meal to make her feel bad.

____ 7. When I want something from my meal,

A.) I do something nice for my meal so he will want to return the favor.

B.) I make my meal feel bad about something so he will feel guilty and want to make it up to me.

C.) I get angry if my meal doesn't know, because he should know me better than that.

D.) I tell him what I want.

E.) I give him hints about what I want.

____ 8. When my meal asks me to do something I don't want to do,

    A.) I tell her I will but then don't do it.

    B.) I do it to make her happy.

    C.) I tell her why I don't feel comfortable doing it.

    D.) I'll do it so I have something to throw in her face when I need something.

    E.) I'll do it but complain about it.

____ 9. When I meet a same-gender attractive, smart, and interesting person,

    A.) I challenge him to show that I'm better than he is.

    B.) I get quiet and just let him talk.

    C.) I make him my new best friend and try to imitate him.

    D.) I point out to people how he isn't really that special.

    E.) I enjoy his company and try to learn something new.

____ 10. I am only happy when

    A.) I'm taking care of myself.

    B.) someone is taking care of me.

    C.) I'm doing fun things with people I love.

    D.) I'm taking care of someone else.

    E.) I'm in a relationship.

Go back and place a score for each of your choices on the line in front of the question's number.

For questions 1 and 6:	For questions 2 and 7:
A = 2 points	A = 4 points
B = 7 point	B = 0 points
C = 10 points	C = 2 points
D = 4 points	D = 10 points

E = 0 points

E = 7 points

For questions 3 and 8:

A = 7 points

B = 4 point

C = 10 points

D = 0 points

E = 2 points

For questions 4 and 9:

A = 0 points

B = 7 points

C = 4 points

D = 2 points

E = 10 points

For questions 5 and 10:

A = 10 points

B = 2 point

C = 7 points

D = 0 points

E = 4 points

Enter your total score here:

My Total Score _____

What Your Score Means

Throughout this book I have talked about being nutritious and making nutritious choices. By "nutritious" I mean "empowered." Your thoughts, emotions, and actions are your power.

Maintaining and using your power properly is the key to finding and keeping a happy, healthy relationship.

Power is often improperly defined as control. Some people call it having the upper hand. It's a big misconception that you need to have control of a relationship to be happy. It is yourself you need to control, not the relationship! Having control of the relationship or your partner is actually a misuse of your power. Giving away control leaves you vulnerable. Either way you'll end up getting hurt. The way to be happy is to accept responsibility for everything you do and respect your partner's thoughts, emotions, and actions. Start by accepting your answers to this quiz.

If you scored 0–19, you're not in control of your power. You're trying to have control. You're using manipulation to get your needs met. You're even being abusive. The wall you have built to protect yourself is only keeping you alone. Your anger is hurting others and pushing them away. It probably scares you to be vulnerable and allow anyone to know your true feelings, but no one can love you unless you're willing to let them. You need to be brave and learn to trust yourself to know when others will not to hurt you. If you treat people with respect and compassion, they will treat you the same way—and you will feel better about it.

Start by doing nothing when you feel you want to control the situation. Push the pause button. Just ask to take a break and walk away to think about it. Tell yourself you are only strong when you control your own actions. Your actions should never hurt or use anyone else. If you need someone to do something for you, ask for his or her help. It will be okay. If that's hard for you, say so. By showing vulnerability, you can make a stronger connection, and others will then be more willing to help you. If they tell you no, don't take it personally. That's just what they're comfortable with; it's not about you. Accept their "no"; don't try to change their answer.

Your boundaries are currently too rigid. The next section, "Your Place Setting," will help you loosen your boundaries to a healthier level.

If you scored 20–37, you're not protecting your power. Your boundaries are too loose. Knowing your inner feelings, wants, needs, and limits, as well as fulfilling and enforcing them without hurting others, is what healthy boundaries are all about. That means finding your true self and protecting it, no matter what, without needing anyone else's approval. It means not letting anyone else change what you know is right for you, as well as not allowing anyone to take you for granted or mistreat you, not even a little bit.

We teach people how to treat us. If someone disrespects you and you allow it to happen without saying anything, you've just taught him or her that that is okay behavior and that they can continue to treat you however they want. If you blame someone else for the things that happen to you, you're giving away your power. But if you calmly express what was not okay with you and request how you'd like to be treated in the future, you'll command respect. It doesn't matter what anyone else does; it only matters how you choose to respond to it.

If you scored 38–57, you're giving away your power. You don't love yourself enough. A person will only think of you in the same way that *you* think of yourself. It's not about what he or she wants, likes, or does. It's all about you! What matters is truly knowing you are amazing and not settling for anyone who doesn't see that. You should be more afraid of losing yourself than of losing any man or woman.

Stop putting your happiness in the hands of someone else. Only you can make you happy. The only way you can be part of a true partnership is by becoming a complete person who functions independently, on your own, without needing a partner to make you whole. That means getting in touch with your inner thoughts and feelings, standing up for yourself, taking responsibility for all your actions, and making conscious, healthy choices. Your first choice must always be to take care of you. When you leave things up to hope, chance, or someone else, you're giving away your power.

If you scored 58–89, you need to own your power. You need to stand up for yourself more. It feels comfortable for you to go along to get along, but that isn't getting your needs met. You have to ask for what you want. No one can fulfill your desires if no one knows what they are. People will have more respect for you—and you'll be more attractive to others—if you voice your opinion and express your thoughts. That doesn't mean you need to be aggressive; instead, just be confident in a gentle but firm manner about who you are and what you want.

Read the section above for scoring 38–57 as, you could also benefit by loving yourself a little more.

If you scored 90–100: You're empowered! You're a superfood; you are using and maintaining your power properly. That's the first step in finding and keeping a well-balanced meal. Healthy people fall in love with positive individuals who love themselves. If you can get into relationships but none have worked out for you yet, you're probably picking the wrong partners.

Food For Thought

You're giving away your power when

- you put your happiness in the hands of someone else,

- you leave things up to hope or chance, or

- you blame someone else for the things that happen to you.

Maintaining your power is about accepting responsibility for everything you do. I mean *everything*. Too many adults don't. Remember when something didn't go right for you as a kid? Your mom would ask, "What happened?" Undoubtedly you'd respond, "I don't know," or "It wasn't me!" or "He made me do it!" Essentially you'd play dumb, deny it, or blame someone else because your brain hadn't fully developed past the "it's all about me" stage yet. How about now? How many of those tactics are you still using today? And how's that working for you?

Now that you're an adult, having it "all about you" can actually be a good thing. But only if that means you're in touch with your inner thoughts and feelings, you take responsibility for all your actions, and you make conscious choices—healthy choices. That means not blaming anyone else for anything. It doesn't matter what they do. It only matters how *you* choose to respond.

Relationships are about choices. You always have a choice.

Even when you feel like things are out of your control, there is always something you can choose to do to make it better for you.

It's the classic case of the glass being half empty or half full. The key to being empowered is knowing that everything in life is about how you choose to view it—and always choosing something positive.

Feeding Yourself

Your first choice must always be to take care of yourself. That is not being selfish; it's being smart. You are no good to anyone else if you aren't whole. That's why on airplanes they tell you to put your own oxygen mask on before helping others. Too many people put all their focus on what their *partner* wants, allowing their own needs to suffer. Even worse, they look to their *partner* to take care of them. They're needy. Either way, you're giving away your power. You'll become unattractive to healthy meals. The word "partner" is supposed to imply an equal, not a dependent. A true partner wants a woman or man he or she can respect.

The only way a relationship can work is if it is a true partnership of two complete people. By a complete person I mean someone who functions independently, on his or her own, without *needing* the other person to make him or her whole. It was a very romantic climax in the movie *Jerry Maguire* when Tom Cruise's character said to Renee Zellweger's character, "You complete me." In reality that's codependence, and it's very unhealthy.

If you're feeling right now that your life won't be complete until you find a man or woman and have a relationship, then you're giving away your power. You're pushing all the good meals away along with it. It didn't really help if you grew up as I did, watching movies like *Cinderella* and *Sleeping Beauty*, in which the fair maiden had no life until the handsome prince rescued her. That was a bad message! Buried deep in your subconscious may be the belief that your happily ever after lies in the hands of Prince Charming. Or that you need to rescue a damsel in distress for her to love you. That's not true! Your happiness is in your hands—in your mind, actually. That's exactly what I'm talking about when I say you need to change your thinking.

It's good to have hope. True hope means you believe in yourself. That's excellent! Just don't just leave your hope hanging out there as a dream; that's putting your power in someone else's hands. Turn your dreams into goals, and use your desire to inspire actions that can help you reach those goals. If you want a quality man or woman, then make your goal about becoming a great partner. Make yourself the best that you can be. Acknowledge that Prince Charming doesn't exist. Decide to become Prince or Princess Self-Empowered.

No one can truly love you until

- you truly love yourself,

- you value who you are and believe in yourself,

- you do all the things you want to do without waiting for someone else, and

- you choose to be happy just being you.

It's perfectly healthy to *want* a man or woman, but that's a whole different energy than *needing* one. Besides, having a full life that he or she has to work a little harder to fit into makes you a much more interesting date. You'll be naturally more selective about who is worthy of your time.

I'm not talking about faking it. Several books have been written advising women to play games in order to catch a man. Men have read them too. These books have created all sorts of dating confusion. Men who have read these books don't know if women are playing hard to get or are just not interested. Women who have read these books end up turning off guys they really liked. For example, I'm sure you've heard that you should only talk on the phone for a certain number of minutes, that a man has to call X number of days in advance if he expects to take a woman out, that you shouldn't see someone more than once a week, or that you shouldn't kiss on the first date. I'm not saying that this kind of advice is bad; in fact, some of it can be really helpful. But you can't do these things just because you were told to. Tricks may help you get the girl or guy, but they most certainly won't help you keep him or her. The real you will emerge eventually as the relationship progresses. You need to *become* the person that does those things naturally because they feel right; because you're an independent, completely nutritious superfood; and because you won't allow anyone to take you for granted or mistreat you—not even a little bit. That's very attractive!

We teach people how to treat us. If someone disrespects you and you allow it to happen without saying anything, you've just taught him or her that it is acceptable behavior and that he or she can continue to behave that way. And that person will indeed continue to do so until he or she loses respect for you and leaves. If you overreact and tell that person off, you've taught him or her that you're not in control of your power. If that person likes drama, he or she will continue to disrespect you, hoping to engage you in future scenes, thus creating a dysfunctional relationship. If someone is healthy, he or she will see your outburst as a huge junk-food flag. He or she will lose interest and move on. However, if you calmly express what was not okay with you and request how you'd like to be treated in the future, you'll command respect. If you don't get respect, then you should lose interest and walk away.

The way to attract and keep a healthy, well-balanced meal is to set your personal bar high and properly enforce your boundaries at all times. That's being empowered.

YOUR PLACE SETTING— HEALTHY BOUNDARIES

Having healthy boundaries means knowing your inner feelings, wants, needs, and limits, as well as fulfilling and enforcing them without hurting others. That means finding your true self and protecting it, no matter what, without needing anyone else's approval. Enforcing healthy boundaries means not letting anyone else change what you know is right for you. That's not always easy. How many times have you been upset with someone and intended to tell him or her about it, only to have your resolve weaken once you were face-to-face? Then, instead of maintaining your power, you allowed the other person to dominate the situation. You got caught up in his or her energy and ignored your own intention, allowing your boundaries to collapse.

Without healthy boundaries, your life and relationships are certain to have problems. Depending on what your childhood was like, you might not have been taught much about boundaries. Most people have never even heard of them.

Children from dysfunctional homes, especially children of abuse—sexual, physical, and emotional—often anesthetize their pain and hide from their feelings by putting their focus outside of themselves. They may frequently develop a fantasy world to escape into, and they often become obsessed with other people, places, or things. Their childhood abuser has taken away their power, and they don't know how to get it back, or that they even have any power in the first place.

Parents who lack boundaries often use their children to fill their own emptiness. This causes the child to feel his or her own needs aren't important because he or she is always focused on pleasing the parent. These children don't develop an individual identity. Since boundaries are usually not taught in school, these children grow up with distorted, underdeveloped, or overdeveloped boundaries. As adults they stay disconnected from their inner selves, ultimately feeling lonely even within relationships.

How do you find your true self if you weren't taught you had one as a child? Typically you look for it in romantic partners. If you don't know how to take care of your own needs, you need someone else to take care of you or tell you what to do. If you're used to taking care of a parent or sibling, then you don't feel complete if you're not taking care of someone else. Either way, this is called codependence. Codependents frequently meld their existence with that of the person they're dating. Have you ever dropped your schedule and your friends to jump into a new lover's life? Then, when someone asks you what you're up to, all you can talk about is him or her. You draw your sense of self from the relationship and how your partner perceives you. I once saw Heather Graham on a late-night talk show, back when she was dating Ed Burns. All she talked about was how great *he* was. I practically screamed at the TV, "You're the one on *The Tonight Show*! I want to hear about *you*, not him!"

Codependents will usually pull you into every aspect of their life immediately. They seem really nice when you first meet, but then they start inviting you out every night. It's too much, too soon. They want to be included in everything you do, and they pout if you want time to yourself. You need to give each other space so you have time to evaluate the relationship and allow real feelings to develop. I once dated a very needy guy who kept asking me out daily, but he always asked me out to do really fun things, so I kept accepting. One night when he was dropping me off, he said, "I miss you already." "You don't give me time to miss you," I replied. That was the truth. I liked him, but he smothered me and suffocated any potential feelings I had before they fully developed. He was basically a between-meal snack. I had told him I was not looking for a relationship; I just wanted to have a little fun. In fact, I told him that many times. He eventually said, "You don't have much tact." "You don't listen," I replied. "Your actions show me that you're ignoring that I don't want to be your exclusive girlfriend." He still didn't hear me, and he got hurt.

When what you want and need starts to get lost in the blender with what your partner wants and needs, it's not a relationship; it's enmeshment. Many people are very comfortable with not knowing where one partner ends and the other begins, but it's unhealthy. Such couples usually consist of two codependent people who have found each other—one needy person loving another needy person. What's wrong with that? It stunts your personal growth. You may end up feeling guilty for wanting to do things without your partner—or overly jealous if he or she wants to do things without you. Then if one leaves, or dies, the other is devastated and unable to function. If they have children, they pass this same dysfunction on to them. Often a needy, codependent person looks for someone who seems independent, but they tend to attract commitmentphobes and end up clinging to, smothering, and trying to control them, thus driving them away. Sound familiar? You read about it in chapter 2, "Binging and Purging," on page 62. It's very common.

Signs of unhealthy boundaries

You move too fast. Rushing into relationships is a frequent occurrence when unhealthy or no boundaries exist. "Love at first sight" is only an expression. It should be "intense attraction at first sight." Love takes time to grow. If you feel love immediately, it's more likely lust, infatuation, or, possibly, the beginning of an addiction to that person.

You're an open book. Revealing too much about yourself too soon is a sign of underdeveloped boundaries. It shouldn't feel okay to give up intimate details about yourself before establishing trust. Trust has to be earned, and that takes time. Knowledge is power. Don't give yours away.

You have a bleeding heart. We've all felt compassion when hearing someone's moving story. But do you feel a need to rescue him or her? Do you want to jump in with everything you have to make it better? You may think you're filling your own emptiness by fixing someone else, but you're usually just neglecting yourself. You're draining your own power.

Those warm, fuzzy feelings you get from rescuing someone else are often mistaken for love. Besides, not everyone wants or is open to being fixed; you may be violating her boundaries. If she does accept your help, it becomes an unequal relationship in which you are giving and she is taking.

Healthy boundaries will prompt you to always take care of your own needs first. You can feel compassion and even be supportive without getting emotionally involved in another's problems. When choosing a partner, you want exactly that—a partner. You do not want a dependent. Choose someone you can respect and with whom you can have a healthy give-and-take. A person with a big problem should be a huge junk-food flag to you. Run in the other direction!

You feel like everything is your fault. Do you feel responsible for your partner's failures, happiness, or unhappiness? Do you feel guilty when they fail? Do you apologize for them or accept the consequences for their bad behavior? Healthy boundaries don't allow you to take responsibility for anyone but yourself. You can't control what anyone else does. You shouldn't try to. Save your power for yourself.

You withhold your feelings. Do you have a hard time expressing what you think and feel? Is it difficult, or even impossible, for you to say "I love you" or even "Thank you"? Do you avoid telling your partner what he or she does that upsets you? Perhaps you feel you're protecting your partner or yourself. But in reality you're setting up future conflict. This is a sign of overdeveloped boundaries. No one can give you what you want if he or she doesn't know what it is.

You're a people-pleaser. When someone asks you to do something, is your immediate response just to please them? Do you find yourself saying yes and then regretting it later? That's because you answered before you thought about your own needs or the consequences of your actions. You need to be a self-pleaser. People should like you or not for who you are, not for what you do for them. It really only matters what *you* think of you.

You don't stand up for yourself. If you hire someone to provide a service for you and he doesn't properly fulfill your expectations, do you call it to his attention and make him correct it? Or do you complain to other people in your life in the hope that someone else will fix it for you? Do you just live with it as it is, constantly reminded that you didn't stand up for yourself? It's your job to take care of you. People will respect you if you hold them accountable for their actions.

You're comfortable with dysfunction. One of the telltale signs of an absence of healthy boundaries is a high tolerance for inappropriate behavior. That's how abusive relationships are allowed to happen. Many women have said, "If he ever hit me, I'd leave," but they don't realize there are other inappropriate actions they shouldn't tolerate either. Some men who have been hit by women have failed to realize that women can be abusive. Things like being yelled at, called names, belittled, ordered around, or intimidated into doing things you don't want to do are all abuse. All of these things are deal-breakers! There are no acceptable excuses.

You're abusive. Women can be equally abusive to men and to other women. Both the abuser and the abused are exhibiting a breakdown of healthy boundaries. As an abuser, you probably have overdeveloped boundaries. You keep yourself safe by building a wall around your heart to shut people and emotions out. You probably don't realize the effect your behavior has on other people or the pain it may cause. You may even blame them for your actions to make yourself feel better, even to the point at which you find yourself saying "You made me do it." Asking for help or saying yes is difficult when you have rigid boundaries. Being manipulative or controlling may feel like the only way to get your needs met. It's not.

You can't say no. Have you ever been abused, or done something you didn't want to do because you couldn't protest it or didn't think you should? If so, you have underdeveloped boundaries. Feeling like you're obligated to do what others want and not being able to say no leaves you unprotected from unhealthy partners. You lack the empowerment to stand up for yourself, so you're leaving yourself open to be manipulated and controlled.

You can't accept no as an answer. Accepting the word "no" is part of having healthy boundaries. When someone tells you no, then the answer is no. Don't use manipulation to get your way. You can't always get what you want. You have to accept other people's boundaries to maintain your power and their respect.

You can't say yes. Do you have a hard time letting others help you or do nice things for you? Have you developed a tough exterior in order to push everyone away? Are intimate feelings scary? If your boundaries are too rigid, you have essentially built a wall around your heart to keep everyone out. You're missing out on some wonderful things in life.

You don't respect others' privacy. Have you ever obtained the password to your lover's e-mail or smartphone and read his messages? Have you looked at his bank statement or other personal information? That is a huge violation of his privacy and trust. Such actions are signs that you have underdeveloped boundaries and that you're giving your power away. You're unnecessarily upsetting yourself because you can't ask your partner about any disturbing information you might find, which may not even be significant. If you have questions about your partner's personal information, then you have to ask him or her directly. If you're not willing to do that, then it's none of your business. Don't snoop.

Missing Boundaries Checklist

___ I have trouble saying no.

___ I go along to get along.

___ I want to rescue others.

___ I have trouble saying yes and letting others get close.

___ I say yes when I mean maybe, or I say maybe when I mean no.

___ My happiness depends on other people.

___ I ignore my own needs to help others.

___ I think others' needs are more important than mine.

___ I feel guilty when others are unhappy.

___ I take on the moods of others.

___ I feel embarrassed by, and responsible for, the behavior of people I'm with.

___ I have trouble asking for what I want or need.

___ I have trouble expressing my opinion.

___ I have trouble standing up for myself or speaking up when something is wrong.

____ I have a high tolerance for inappropriate behavior.

____ I get involved with people who are bad for me.

____ I read my lover's e-mail.

____ I feel responsible for my partner's failures, happiness, or unhappiness.

____ I'm an open book, revealing too much about myself to mere acquaintances.

____ I feel love very quickly when I'm attracted to someone.

____ I try to control others to get what I want.

____ I push my views and desires on others.

____ I feel uncomfortable if I'm not just like others.

____ I'm unsure of who my true self is.

How to Develop Healthy Boundaries

Begin by recognizing that you have a right to possess boundaries. All of the people in your life must respect your boundaries, or they should not be part of your life. That includes parents, siblings, and friends.

You should now be starting to see how healthy boundaries work and what might be missing for you. By becoming aware of any statement above that you put a check next to, you've taken the first step toward change.

> You can't blame someone else for violating your boundaries.
>
> It's up to you to enforce them and teach people how to treat you.

Try to check in with how you're feeling about everything in your life. Notice how you're treated, spoken to, and valued. Try being aware of boundaries you should have with regard to other people. It might be hard with long-standing relationships, but you'll gain more respect as you start to speak up. Say "I don't like that" or "That makes me uncomfortable" when someone is violating what should be a boundary. You have to claim your power. Be assertive. But don't be aggressive. No need to raise your voice.

If you have a hard time saying no, try saying "I'll get back to you." That will give you a little more time to find the courage to say no. The same goes for saying yes.

It might help to think of yourself as a small child, but play the role of the parent protecting that "inner child." You wouldn't allow a child to be pushed around, or yelled at, would you? By protecting your inner child, you'll be teaching everyone in your life how to treat you. If you enforce your boundaries, they will be respected! Communication is always the key.

Get In Touch with Your True Self.

Your true self = your inner thoughts and emotions

Your inner thoughts and emotions = feelings, beliefs, values, likes, dislikes, wants, needs, intuitions, and goals

Identifying Your True Self

Take your time writing out the honest answers to each of these questions exploring your emotional, physical, and sexual self. Be very specific. Update your list regularly as you discover new things about yourself.

1. What are your moral principles? What core beliefs do you have about life and your participation in it?

2. What do you need? What is absolutely necessary for your survival and well-being? List everything from good nutrition to respect. Include things that you're not currently giving yourself but that you know you should be.

3. What do you like? What brings you pleasure and happiness?

4. What do you dislike? What do you, or should you, refuse to do no matter what? List both trivial and significant things.

5. What are your goals? Where would you like to be two years from now? Five years from now? Ten years? Twenty years?

Know your specific emotional, physical, and sexual needs, desires, and limits, and never compromise them. Protect your true self at all times. When you can truly trust yourself to enforce your boundaries and take care of you, then you can function in a healthy relationship. You'll also then be able to recognize and attract a healthy partner.

You'll know you're in a healthy relationship when

- both you and your partner consciously choose how much to loosen your individual boundaries to allow intimacy with each other—you should leave or stop every situation that makes you uncomfortable;

- you respect your partner's needs, feelings, and values even if they are different from your own;

- you're able to say and accept hearing no in response to another's desires;

- you're able to say yes appropriately;

- you don't allow anyone to control you, and you don't try to control anyone; and,

- you accept your partner for himself or herself, as he or she is.

When healthy boundaries exist, you can allow your partner to be himself or herself and do things on his or her own, without your supervision—as you will want your partner to do for you.

Putting yourself first

Contrary to what you were probably taught, a little selfishness and self-indulgence is a good thing. It's actually a requirement. You need to put yourself first. Only after you have taken care of your own needs can you decide if you want to help someone else. Decide by asking two questions:

1. Can this person help himself or herself?

2. Will I resent giving up my time, energy, resources, money, or whatever it may require to help him or her?

Example: The person you're dating asks you to drive her to the airport at 5:00 a.m. on Tuesday. Before you respond, ask yourself a few questions. Will you have enough time to get to work if you drive her? Will you get enough sleep? Does she have any other way to get there? How will you feel if you drive her? Will you resent it? Will you expect something in return? If so, negotiate that upfront—if you don't, you can't expect anything. When you honestly answer these questions, then you'll know how to appropriately answer. You'll have put yourself first.

Furthermore, you don't need to take on the world's problems, or even your partner's. If she had a bad day, you can (and probably should) sympathize without having to literally "feel her pain" or try to save her. You're not responsible for your partner or whatever she is feeling. It's not your fault. You'll actually be more helpful to your partner if you can remain calm and somewhat detached. Allow her to feel what she is feeling and just be supportive.

Self-Aware, Not Self-Absorbed

Being self-absorbed or narcissistic is a huge turnoff. Healthy selfishness does not mean self-righteousness. It doesn't mean you're better than anyone else or entitled to anything more than he or she is. You should never push yourself on another in any way or use anyone else to get your needs met. You should never hurt someone else to get what you want. You have to ask for permission when you desire something. You need to respect that everyone is an individual and should have his or her own healthy boundaries too.

Don't be a know-it-all. It's not your place to correct someone else on his or her behavior unless it's hurting or upsetting you. Even then you have to take responsibility by saying something like "It hurts me when you do that" or "I feel scared when you act that way." It has to be about you and your feelings, not about what the other person is doing.

Don't Crowd the Cook

I feel I should mention that personal space is frequently overlooked or violated. Imagine that you and all other people are in permeable bubbles. You can't enter anyone else's bubble, and no one else can enter yours unless invited. That means you should not stand too close to others or touch them in any way if they have not made it perfectly clear that it's okay with them. This includes pregnant women's bellies! Just because there is a baby inside doesn't give you the right to touch the mother. You are the keeper of your bubble. If someone makes you uncomfortable, say so. You can be nice about it, but you need to be very clear where you end and everyone else begins.

Finally, healthy boundaries should also be flexible. They'll help you let the good things in while keeping the bad things out. They help you set the pace for the beginning of a relationship by exploring how and if your boundaries fit with your partner's. When you do choose an appropriate partner, flexible boundaries will allow you to get close to him or her. You can decide how and when you want to talk or be touched, how and when you want to let him into your life, and how and when you don't. It is all up to you!

Checklist for Healthy Boundaries

- ✓ Take care of yourself and your needs.
- ✓ Maintain your individual identity.
- ✓ Take responsibility for your own thoughts, feelings, ideas, and actions.
- ✓ Don't be inappropriately influenced by or responsible for others.
- ✓ Don't allow yourself to be controlled, manipulated, or enmeshed with others.
- ✓ Don't try to control, manipulate, or hurt anyone else to get what you want.

When you implement healthy, flexible boundaries, you'll feel really good about yourself. Self-esteem commands respect. It's very attractive. Love yourself and you will find a well-balanced meal.

By Roger Disney www.RogerDisney.com

CLEANING OUT YOUR REFRIGERATOR

There are typically two different ways single people stock their refrigerators. You either don't cook and therefore only keep the basics, such as beverages and maybe condiments from when you ordered out, or you're a home gourmet (frozen foods count) and thus keep the fridge fully stocked. Either way, you probably keep some leftovers, and if you don't clean out your refrigerator regularly, things start to accumulate and go bad.

The same thing is true for your psyche. As you go from relationship to relationship, or even while you stay in the same one for a long time, you amass memories and behaviors. Each partner triggers your past emotions and reactivates your unhealed wounds, most of which are unconscious wounds from childhood. You then react with conditioned

186

responses that have nothing to do with your partner. All these imprints of emotions, scars, and actions start to clutter up your brain, causing your thinking to get fuzzy like that old tomato in your fridge. They make it more difficult for you to respond appropriately to what's going on in the present moment. This clutter is known as baggage. It leaves you no room for anyone else. You need to clean out your head once in a while so you can clear away the obstructions and appreciate what you have.

Okay, so now that I've grossed you out by causing you to think of your head as a rotting fridge, are you motivated to do some cleaning? Don't worry; you won't need rubber gloves for this disinfecting. It's time to roll up your sleeves and reevaluate how you approach dating and relationships.

The first step in cleaning out your refrigerator is to take everything out to see what you have. Then you can evaluate what to keep and what to throw out. You'll use your past partners as a mirror to help you to see your issues. Then I'll help you recognize the things that trigger you, so you can consciously change your responses. I'll help you examine and acknowledge the things you do well, because you have to appreciate yourself before anyone else can. Depending on your personality type, one of these exercises will be more important for you. But you'll find value in both.

Laying It All Out on the Table

To have a good relationship, you need to know everything you do to contribute, whether good, bad, or ugly.

If you're the kind of person who finds it hard to hear nice things about yourself, or if you're a people-pleaser who is always doing nice things for others, then this exercise will be important for you.

Table One: What I've Done Right in Relationships

Draw a line down the center of a piece of paper and write "What I Did" on the left side and "Why I Did It" on the right side. Follow the guide on the next page. Use extra pages if you need them.

What I Did	Why I Did it
1. List all the things you have done that made you or your partner happy.	Write what prompted you to do each thing or what you hoped to achieve.
Example A: I made my boyfriend's favorite meal for dinner.	I knew he was having a tough day. Or: I wanted to butter him up so I could borrow his car.
Example B: I let her go out with her friends without arguing, acting jealous or pouting.	I wanted to show her I trust her. Or: I wanted to have dinner with my ex-girlfriend.
2. List how you stood up for yourself and took care of your own needs.	Fill in what prompted you to do each thing or what you hoped to achieve.
Example C: I told him it upset me when he smiled at other girls.	It was building up inside me and I didn't want to eventually explode.

Now is the time to come clean. If you apologized for something you did that upset your partner, think about why you apologized.

- Did you know you were wrong and so think it was the right thing to apologize?

- Was it partly to avoid conflict?

- Was it so you could get something in return?

- Did you feel that you were right but didn't feel it was worth the argument that you knew would follow?

- Do you hate arguing and would rather keep the peace at any cost?

Really search your feelings to find the truth about why you do the things you do. Then, whatever your truth is, write it down.

Common Ingredients

When you have finished your list, go back and look for patterns. Check any patterns below that apply:

_____You frequently put your needs second for the benefit of your partner.

_____You feel lost if you're not doing something for someone else.

_____You frequently do nice things as manipulation for your own gain.

_____You do nice things because it makes you feel good.

Do you stand up for yourself? Do you take care of your own needs? If not, you may be taken for granted or taken advantage of. There is such a thing as being too nice. You have to demonstrate self-respect. It's not good for you or your relationship if you're always neglecting your own needs to accommodate your partner's. You have to take care of yourself first! When you do, you exude confidence and demand respect. No relationship can succeed without respect. Confidence is very attractive.

What If My List Is Short?

Perhaps you don't have many things on the list of things you have done for your partner or partners. That could indicate too much self-importance and selfishness, which is a manifestation of low self-esteem. Frequently this is a result of putting too much emphasis on competition and trying to be better than everyone else. It's really just insecurity. All people are created equal, but let's face it; some people get dealt a better hand to start with. That can be hard to deal with if you don't think you were allotted a good hand. However, what you do with what you have is what makes you special. We all love the story of the underdog who builds a wonderful life for himself or herself. The underdog is always more lovable than the enviable person who seems to naturally have it all. There will always be people who seem "better" than you, just as there will always be people who you'll seem "better" than. That's life. Don't put unnecessary stress on yourself.

- Don't compare yourself to anyone else.

- You should only hold yourself up to being your own personal best.

- Appreciate others for who they are, and let them inspire you.

- Learn from others.

- Don't disparage others.

- Don't compete with your partner. Competition within a relationship can kill it.

Perhaps your list is short because you have difficulty acknowledging yourself for those things you did right or because you feel you have no good qualities to bring to a relationship. Nonsense; of course you do! Everyone has at least one good aspect. Really bad people don't ever think they're bad, so you are absolutely not bad. You do need to find out why you feel so inadequate. If someone in your life has told you that you are nothing, that person lied! Furthermore, that person is bad for you. Everyone *is* special in his or her own unique way. You need to find a way to believe this for yourself. If you're reading this book and putting in the effort to examine yourself and do these exercises, that's evidence right there that you are someone special.

What Do My Patterns Mean?

If you noted a pattern of doing nice things for your partner with a motive for your own gain, that is a sign that you're a manipulator. Do you feel like you need to have the control in a relationship, or like you won't be loved if you can't control your partner? Control is another sign of low self-esteem and insecurity. If you give up control for trust and honesty, you're more likely to find real love and your partner will be more likely to want to do things for you.

If you do nice things for your partner just because it makes you feel good, then make sure you *truly* have no expectations from it. Always remember that your partner didn't ask you to do it. You can't throw a kind act in his face as leverage when you want something from him. You can't guilt your partner into doing things for you. A completely unconditional act is exactly that—unconditional. Just don't be taken advantage of; make sure it's in an equal relationship. Don't do unconditional things for undeserving or unappreciative people.

Grade-A Inspections

Lastly, with all this talk about lacking self-esteem, look back over your list and pat yourself on the back right now for all the things you did right. Really celebrate them! A great way to boost your self-esteem is to acknowledge yourself for your accomplishments. This is a perfect opportunity to focus on all your positive deeds.

Today's kids receive tremendous acknowledgment from their families, teachers, and coaches. For every little thing they do, they hear "Good job!" or "That was awesome!" They get ribbons just for playing in a game. This can be excellent for building self-esteem. But previous generations weren't as nurtured. Most of our parents didn't have the benefit of *Oprah* or *The Super Nanny* to teach them good parenting skills. How much acknowledgment did you get?

I'm always amazed at how many adults are so genuinely touched when I compliment their accomplishments, usually because nobody else ever has. For some, it's even uncomfortable to hear me say "I'm proud of you" or to suggest they be proud of themselves. It's unfamiliar dialogue. Their familiar, negative internal voice is easier to believe. Take the time now to acknowledge yourself for the things you do well.

Silence Your Food Critic

Society loves to tear everybody down—ever read the tabloids? I suspect that might be because people are trying to feel better about themselves. For many individuals, no one is harder on them than they are. Far too many good people have a brutal internal critic that beats them up horribly. Do you have one? If you do, it's time to shut that critic up!

One client I had was particularly hard on himself. His inner voice was incredibly mean if he failed to be perfect at everything. Since no one can possibly be perfect at everything, he was beating himself up most of the time. He was quite successful in his business. But when I complimented him for achieving so much without a formal education, he was utterly speechless. He confessed he felt I was lying. Essentially it didn't matter to him what anyone else said, because he couldn't truly believe he possessed any positive traits. No wonder he couldn't find a partner. If he didn't like himself, how could anyone else like him? I asked him what it would feel like to give himself permission to just be average. What could he do to reward himself for even trivial accomplishments? He thought these were interesting ideas.

As he began to recognize his self-defeating thoughts, he told me he was developing a good "defense attorney." I pointed out that you have to be accused of doing something wrong to need a defense attorney. Since he had not, I proposed he imagine an inner cheerleader instead—a positive voice cheering him on and congratulating him on anything and everything he did. He liked that idea. So did I. That's why I'm passing it on to you. My goal is to turn all inner critics into supportive cheerleaders. Will you join me in my mission?

Acknowledgment doesn't come easily in the real world, if at all. It's your job to give it to yourself. Every time you complete something from your to-do list, say to yourself "Good girl!" or "Great job!"—especially if it was something you had been putting off. If you didn't manage to check off all your tasks, ask yourself what got in the way. Forgive yourself. Then put it on a realistic schedule for when it can be completed.

Most importantly, the next time you catch yourself thinking negative or self-deprecating thoughts, let your cheerleader interrupt. Your thoughts create your reality, so make sure your reality is positive and supportive of you.

Nobody is perfect! Stop being so hard on yourself!

Most people hate seemingly perfect people anyway. When you perceive that someone is worse off than you, neurons are triggered in your brain that literally make you feel better about yourself.[23] So if you

[23] Goleman, Daniel. *Social Intelligence: The New Science of Human Relationships.* New York: Bantam Books, 2006.

think being perfect will make everyone else love you, that's probably not the case. You're putting an unnecessary burden on yourself.

A reasonable quest for perfection can be a good thing if it makes you stay committed to your goals and work hard to achieve them. But when perfectionism becomes obsessive, it can cause you to ignore your basic needs. While you're trying to be perfect, you're most likely ignoring your true feelings. You may develop an all-or-nothing attitude that tells you, "If it's not perfect, it's useless." This frequently leads to procrastination because you're afraid to fail. Putting too much importance on being perfect drains your energy. All that negative thinking causes unhappiness and, frequently, depression.

When it comes to love and romance, perfectionism usually creates unrealistic expectations, which puts too much of a strain on your relationship. Most perfectionists are hypersensitive to criticism, so accepting responsibility is next to impossible for them. If you're identifying with this, set a goal for yourself to start saying you're sorry. I promise you, you'll get much more pleasant results if you can admit it when you're wrong and apologize. It takes much less energy than defending yourself. It's so much easier for someone to love you if you're showing vulnerability than if you want to fight.

Table Two: What I've Done Wrong in Relationships

How many times have you wished you could go back and do something over again? Well, most behavior does get repeated from partner to partner unless you make a conscious effort to change it. This is your opportunity to fix the things you wish you could, or at least stop beating yourself up about them by preparing not to repeat them in the future. Keeping secrets does more damage than you think.

Divide a piece of paper into three equal parts by drawing two vertical lines. Write "What I Did" on the left side, "Why I Did it" in the middle, and "What I Could Have Done Differently" on the right side. Be sure to include anything that you have never admitted to anyone. Be honest. No one but you ever needs to see this list. You'll feel some of the weight lifting as you write each item down. Follow the guide below. Use extra pages if you need them.

What I Did	Why I Did it	What I Could Have Done Differently
1. List the arguments you started or perpetuated, as well as the times you lost your temper, or over-reacted.	Write what caused you to do it, how you felt, what you were reacting to and why you did what you did. Don't blame anyone else.	Write what you think you could have done to make it right, or what you hope to do the next time it happens.
Example: I burst into her apartment and threw a vase across the room. It smashed into pieces.	I was angry because I thought she lied to me. I wanted to hurt her like she hurt me. I felt jealous and insecure.	I could have calmed down and asked her where she had been. I should have shared how I was feeling.

2. List any manipulations, accusations, or intimidations, and times when you used or withheld sex to control or shut out your partner.

| Example: I told Jerry the guy he thinks wants me would be at a friend's birthday dinner to get him to go with me. | I was angry he didn't want to go. I hate going out alone and I wanted him to pay for me. I was trying to make him jealous. | I could have been honest with Jerry. I should have just gone to the party with my girlfriends. |

3. List any disappointments you created, and times you acted with negligence (hurt someone because of your own carelessness).

4. List any mean things you said, and names you called your partner.

5. List feelings you withheld (didn't communicate), and times you withdrew in stony silence.

6. List betrayals, infidelities and lies.

7. List anything at all that, somewhere inside, you know you didn't do right.

> By "wrong" I mean "not in the best interest of the relationship."
>
> This list is not intended to make you feel bad about yourself or blame or punish yourself. It's intended to make you aware of your contribution to the failure of the relationship so you can learn from past mistakes.
>
> In doing this exercise you *cannot* blame someone else for anything.
>
> No one else can ever make you do anything. Even if you're angry because he or she lied or cheated on you, you always have a choice in how you respond.
>
> You'll feel better if you own up to your actions.

This is a chance to rid yourself of any guilt you may feel about anything you've done, or maybe didn't do, in past relationships. Guilt is an effective warning signal to alert you that there is some work you need to do internally. If you don't do that work to turn off the signal, it starts to cause problems. When harbored or habitual, guilt is a destructive emotion that can hold you back from being happy or succeeding. Constantly beating yourself up causes you to be withdrawn, more critical, and less open. Don't be hard on yourself. Blame isn't good for anyone; taking responsibility is. Making mistakes helps us learn and can actually make us stronger. You can release your guilt by saying "I did this, and I'm sorry. I'm going to learn from it and try not to do it again." Writing it down on paper starts the process of change. As you record each incident, acknowledge that this is the beginning of forgiving yourself.

Most importantly, don't beat yourself up over any of the things you write down. This exercise is largely about forgiving yourself. Remember, nobody's perfect. The past is the past; it's all good if you can learn from it and grow. Forgiveness doesn't mean you condone or excuse what you did, or that you should forget it. Acknowledge it and examine it; you'll learn from it and move on. If there is any incident that continues to nag at you, then you have to take action to make it right. That may mean apologizing to the person you hurt (if it's appropriate to do so), listening to the pain you caused, or doing nice things for anyone involved. Tell someone you trust; talking about it can give you a different perspective and help to release your guilt.

It may not be appropriate to apologize to someone you've wronged if he or she is not aware of it. For example, it might not be a good idea to tell someone if you slept with his or her husband or wife. Sometimes what a certain individual doesn't know won't hurt him or her but may still hurt you. If you have a constant critical voice in your head, try countering it with positive affirmations.

Note: If you're reading this and thinking, "I don't feel guilty about anything. I'm not the one who does things wrong in relationships; it's usually my partner." Well it's good you don't feel guilty, but everyone makes mistakes. As perfect as you may feel, you're not. Nobody is. In fact, you probably need this exercise the most. To get along well with others, you need to be able to admit your mistakes. It really does take two to make a relationship work. If your relationships were working, you wouldn't be reading this book. At the very least, you're choosing the wrong partners.

Recurring Ingredients

When you've finished this list, go back and look for recurring responses, behaviors, and actions, such as losing your temper, lying, blaming, etc. If you've repeated similar behavior frequently, then those behaviors are what you will need to focus on.

Sometimes once you become aware of something, simply making a conscious effort to change it is enough. However, most of our behaviors are deeply rooted from childhood. If you can pinpoint where a behavior originated, then you can start to understand it and you'll have a better chance of changing it. For example, if your mother blamed you for a lot of things as a child, then as an adult you're likely to be very defensive or feel as if everything is your fault. If your parents argued a lot and there was a lot of yelling in your home, then you're likely to respond with inappropriate anger or by shutting down and keeping it bottled up inside. Neither is good for you.

By doing this exercise, you should become aware of the issues you need to focus on. That's the first step in healing. Perhaps you could tell a few of your friends and family members about the behaviors you're trying to change, and invite them to gently call you on it when you exhibit that behavior. You might have to fight the instinct to defend yourself when they do. If you slip, just apologize. Thank them for their help and acknowledge you're trying to change; it will help you grow. They'll likely be supportive of the new you. One of the most frustrating things about positively changing who you are is when friends and family assume you are still the same. Involving them in your growth can garner new respect; it might even be good for them, too.

Now that you're aware of some of your issues, it's up to you to learn more about handling them. There are some great books in the resources list on page 213 that can help you with anger management, handling manipulation and codependence, discovering your childhood issues, or whatever behavioral problem is specific to you.

Doing the Dishes: In Conclusion

After you have finished both exercises, write down the things you've learned about patterns in your behavior.

- List the things that trigger you and how you want to respond.

- List the things you no longer wish to do.

- List the things you will start to do differently in your future relationships.

It may be helpful to keep in mind that you are what you meet, meaning that when you clean up your actions and reactions, you'll attract a healthier partner.

If you previously blamed others for why you did things, I hope you now see how much better your relationships will be by accepting all the responsibility for your actions. It's hard to feel open to someone who is always blaming you for things that aren't your fault, isn't it? When things are your fault, doesn't it feel better to be forgiven than to be blamed?

If you have previously blamed yourself for everything, I hope you now recognize the need to take better care of yourself. The section on boundaries should have been important for you.

Checklist for keeping your refrigerator clean

✓ Make a resolution for yourself to own up to your actions and stop blaming your partner(s).

✓ Make a resolution to always check in with what you're truly feeling. Your behavior reflects your mind-set. When you're in tune with your feelings, you can make good choices. When you're not in tune with your feelings, things usually get out of control.

✓ Consult your new behavior lists often to remind you how you're trying to change.

Example: If you're feeling irritable, try to pinpoint why that is. If you can recognize it's because you were hoping to go to the gym today but too many things kept coming up and stopping you, then when the fifth person of the day (who just happens to be your partner) asks you to do something, you won't snap at him or her. Or if you wanted to have sex with your partner last night but it didn't happen, don't pick fights about household chores to vent your frustration. If you make it a habit to check in with your true feelings, you'll make conscious decisions to take care of your own needs instead. If you feel something festering, ask yourself what will make you feel better. When your first impulse is to take your partner's head off, don't forget to wait ten seconds to respond. Remember, the emotional response center in our brain reacts to an event first and has no editor; the result most likely won't be good. By waiting a minute, you give the more reasoning center of your brain time to engage, which will produce a more appropriate response. Press the pause button. Ask yourself where your emotional urge is coming from, and you'll most likely respond differently. Awareness really does help.

Now that you've cleaned out your refrigerator, and reevaluated your approach, let's take a look at the items you should have in your fridge.

RELATIONSHIP PYRAMID

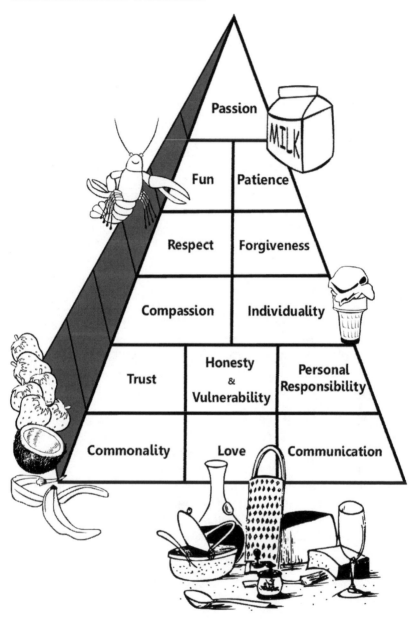

As you look at the relationship pyramid, I hope you now have a better understanding of the nutritious behavior you can use to fortify all your meals—most importantly the one you're serving. A healthy, well-balanced meal has three primary components; these are the base of the relationship pyramid: commonality, love, and communication. All three need to work in harmony for your relationship to succeed. They are the foundation that allows you to reach the upper pyramid levels, the elements of emotional intimacy. Most people know there has to be love. Even if they're not good at communication, they understand it's important. When I tell clients about the three critical elements, I frequently hear "Commonality—that's what we were missing."

Commonality

Commonality means you have the same values, desires, and opinions about life. If you don't agree on what's ethically acceptable or share common life goals, then you cannot create a harmonious partnership. Like attracts like. For example, if your partner uses illegal drugs and you faithfully abide by the law, then you will not be a good match. If having children 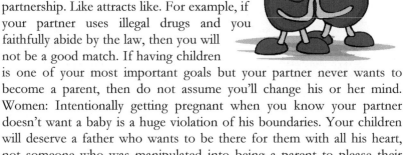 is one of your most important goals but your partner never wants to become a parent, then do not assume you'll change his or her mind. Women: Intentionally getting pregnant when you know your partner doesn't want a baby is a huge violation of his boundaries. Your children will deserve a father who wants to be there for them with all his heart, not someone who was manipulated into being a parent to please their mother.

As you learned in the "Heartburn" section of chapter 1, on page 41, one of the biggest mistakes you can make is thinking you can change someone's mind after he or she has flat-out told you what he or she wants and feels. Save your precious time and energy by just believing what he or she tells you. People don't change unless they want to. The more you push them to change, the more they are going to resent you. If you do manage to get them to agree to what you want, you run a risk of killing any love they feel for you. You have to let people be who they are. It's much easier to just acknowledge that you both want different things or have a incompatible views of life. Let go so you can find a better match.

Another big mistake people make is trying to change who they are to please a lover. This doesn't work. The other person will perceive you as a pushover, which will kill all the attraction he or she feels for you. More importantly, you'll be giving away your power. You'll end up compromising your values, sacrificing your needs, or creating a phony sense of self. Your partner should love you for you. Be proud of who you are. If he doesn't appreciate that, then he is not the right choice for you.

Of course it's nice if your partner inspires you to be a better person—to act more ethically or take better care of yourself. Just like Jack Nicholson's great line, "You make me want to be a better man" to Helen Hunt's character in *As Good As It Gets*. Just make sure you use your boundaries to protect yourself at all times. If you go against your true self to please a partner, you'll end up hating either your partner or yourself. Neither is good.

Statistics indicate that about 50 percent of all first marriages fail. The median age for women marrying today is 25.8; for men it's 28.3.[24] I think those failed couples got married too young and grew in different directions. You have to know who you are before you can effectively choose a life partner. New studies have found that the reasoning and decision-making centers of our brain don't even fully develop until we're twenty-five years old.[25] How can you make a reasonable decision about the rest of your life prior to age twenty-five? You will definitely change a lot throughout your twenties. I think your twenties are a time to date and discover a variety of things. Boyfriends and girlfriends can certainly introduce you to a lot. One partner could be a boater, another a triathlete, and another into the arts and culture. Live your life, and explore different things. Don't commit to marriage until you are certain of who your true self is and that you can protect it.

---

[24] Casey E. Copen, Kimberly Daniels, Jonathan Vespa, and William Mosher, "First Marriages in the United States: Data From the 2006–2010 National Survey of Family Growth," *National Health Statistics Reports*, no. 49 (2012). Accessed December 9, 2012 at www.cdc.gov/nchs/data/nhsr/nhsr049.pdf.

[25] "Brain Maturity Extends Well Beyond Teen Years," *Tell Me More*, National Public Radio, October 10, 2011, radio broadcast, mp3, http://www.npr.org/templates/story/story.php?storyId=141164708.

Commonality is one of the vital elements of a healthy relationship. It's the first one you need to establish when you're choosing a person to be your partner. You should now have an idea of what your personal requirements are from your healthy-meal flags, favorite meal quiz, and true-self exercise. Use them to compile one master list of the characteristics you require in a mate—your perfect-mate profile. That is your new paradigm. Don't alter it or settle for less. It's doesn't matter how attracted to him or her you are; if he or she doesn't match your requirements, you shouldn't get involved. You'll be saving yourself a lot of future heartache.

Love

The next essential healthy-meal element is love. Love can conquer all. It sounds so simple, right? Wrong! One of the hardest concepts to accept is that loving someone just isn't enough. Too many men and women allow themselves to become doormats because they believe true love will triumph. They're convinced that there will never be another person they will love as much, so they hang on to their relationship even when their love is not *appropriately* returned or appreciated. They make all sorts of excuses for their partner's bad or even abusive behavior, all in the name of love. But that's not real love. That's the kind of dysfunction that gives love a bad name. Love isn't supposed to hurt. True love feels great! It helps keep you happy and in good health, and it helps you feel empowered.

So what exactly is true love? To start with, it's mutual between both partners. Each genuinely cares about the other's well-being and happiness. In a real partnership, it's never "all about you." True lovers respect each other's feelings and keep intimate information in confidence; they don't want or need to share everything about the relationship with their friends and family. They allow their partner to be who she is and do the things she enjoys, whether or not that includes them. They trust each other to always value the relationship. That includes being faithful and acting in their partner's best interest. When you truly love someone, you never want to hurt her or cause her pain.

You can tell you're truly in love when simply being in your partner's company comforts you. You feel content and good about yourself. That comfort carries over even when you're not together. You don't need to be with your partner all the time, but you're proud to include him in anything that you do. Your partner is your best friend. He is the first person you want to share news with, good or bad, and you can talk to him about anything. When love is right, it's easy.

When should you first say "I love you?" Trust your instincts. If you're feeling it in the first week or so, realize that your feelings are probably lust or infatuation, not true love. If you say those three little words too quickly, a healthy partner will think you're unhealthy, perhaps even a love addict (which you might be). However, if you've been spending a lot of time together and all the above-mentioned qualities are there, your partner probably does share your feelings. I still believe the man should say it first. But if you are a woman and you really want to tell him, you could start by saying "I think I'm falling in love with you" and see how he responds.

If you bring this up with your partner and his or her body language gets stiff and he or she seems uncomfortable, let him or her bring it up the next time. If your partner chooses not to see you again after you reveal your loving feelings, then he or she is saving you a lot of precious time, as he or she is definitely not the one for you. Maintain your power! Most likely your partner will be relieved you brought it up first and seize the opportunity to tell you his or her true feelings.

Now all this isn't to say true love is just a fairy tale and doesn't ever require work. It just shouldn't feel like hard labor. You should never feel like you're the one exerting all the effort or jumping through hoops to make it work. It should be a mutual attempt. Love may not conquer all, but true love will motivate you to stick with it through any tough times. It's the foundation that connects you together.

How Do You Keep Love Alive?

Simple acknowledgment goes a long way toward fostering love and keeping your partner happy. People need to feel desired and wanted. Once you're in a healthy, committed relationship, share any loving thought that goes through your head. Compliment your partner frequently—make it a habit. Tell her she's beautiful or sexy. Tell him he's sexy, handsome, or smart. Feed his ego! I was once speaking with a client who is an Ivy League–educated, beautiful, successful, and independent woman. She was telling me about something her boyfriend shared with her, and she said, "Well, I didn't need to feed his ego." "Why not?" I asked, "Men are like little boys. They want to impress you. Let them." She laughed and said, "Wow, I never thought about it, but that makes sense." Let your man or woman know how much you appreciate him or her. Your partner is not your competition. Leave a sexy note on his pillow, or send her a greeting card. A thank-you or congratulations for a job well done is always nice. Remember, energy is contagious; it will make it easier for your admiration to be returned.

Sharing your loving thoughts is a great way to establish or rekindle emotional intimacy. Your partner should feel like she can come to you with anything. Let her know you'll always be empathetic and compassionate. Make your partner feel assured that you won't judge or discount her feelings, and she will naturally feel close to you.

Note that I'm not talking about smothering your partner with obsessive love. Don't overwhelm him with your feelings and appear needy; that will drive your partner away. Express your feelings in moderation and with power. Show your partner you want, but do not need, him. Save saying "I love you" for important moments when it will mean something special. If you say it all the time, it starts to sound mechanical and less authentic. You never want to be phony; just be yourself.

Communication

The third essential element of a healthy meal is communication. Throughout this book I've been talking about how to communicate effectively. Being nutritious is largely about how well you express your feelings. Your delivery makes all the difference. Poor communication using drama and manipulation will destroy love and leave you lonely. With the right tools and a little practice, true love can blossom.

Some of us are naturally more dramatic than others. For some people, everything is simply more interesting with a theatrical flair. Drama queens, they're called—sometimes affectionately, and sometimes in frustration. Others only become dramatic when they don't get their way or when they get angry. It's a tactic most effectively used by two-year-olds. Toddlers don't know yet how to use words, so screaming and throwing temper tantrums is the only way for them to get their needs met. But it's never pleasant to be on the receiving end of a temper tantrum—especially from someone who's old enough to know better. A nutritious superfood is smart about communicating. He or she knows that drama will destroy his or her relationship.

The first step in creating a drama-free relationship is taking responsibility for your own behavior, thoughts, and feelings. It's all about you maintaining your power. The "Constipation" section of chapter 1, on page 24, gave you guidelines for healthy communication. Let's review what you've learned.

Checklist for Good Communication

✓You can't blame others for what they do; you can only take responsibility for how you choose to respond.

✓You have to make requests for what you'd like in the future. Never make demands.

✓If someone can't or won't give you what you want, you have to accept his boundaries. You must never manipulate anyone to get your way.

✓You have to ask for what you want. No one can give it to you if she doesn't know what it is. Don't beat around the bush using hints or assume she should instinctually know without you telling her.

✓You should check in with yourself to decide how you're truly feeling before you choose to discuss anything with your partner. Check in with your friends first if you think they will help.

✓Never ambush your partner with your feelings. Make an appointment to talk about important matters.

✓Don't be competitive. You want to be a partner, not an adversary.

The Recipe: As I Eat Healthier, I Attract Healthier Eaters

The concept for using a food metaphor to help identify relationship problems was born out of the reality that what you put in is what you get out. Whatever you put into your body will start to affect you. Alcohol, drugs, health food, junk food, toxins—they all affect your overall health and state of mind. Those you choose to spend time with and get involved with affect your health and state of mind too. Always protect your heart and take the time to allow the relationship to grow. There are all sorts of people with personality disorders, fears, issues, and unavailability that will try to rush you into a relationship. Enforce strong boundaries and set a pace that feels right for you. Anything worth having is worth waiting for.

One of the great things about doing all this work on yourself (besides getting healthier) is that as you begin to identify your own issues, it will become easier for you to see everyone else's issues too. What used to seem appealing will become very unattractive, and it will be easier for you to make healthier choices. I hope that when you spot junk-food in the future, you will choose to resist any temptation. You are now a nutritious superfood—an empowered man or woman.

Doggie Bag
Giving Up Junk-Food Relationships

➡ Be Prince or Princesses Self-Empowered!

➡ Enforce healthy boundaries.

➡ Trust your instincts!

➡ You are what you think you are. Think positively!

➡ Like attracts like. Be a well-balanced meal and you'll attract one.

➡ Don't give your milk away carelessly.

➡ Communicate effectively.

➡ Use the pyramid to know when to allow yourself to be vulnerable in order to achieve emotional intimacy.

Quiz: Hearty Appetite or Something to Tide You Over

Are You Ready For a Well-Balanced Meal, or Just a Dessert (Casual Dating)? Answer each question below according to how you honestly feel, *not* with what you believe the right answer should be. Circle the letter of the answer you choose. Don't worry about your score yet.

___ 1. When on a date, I might

A.) subtly glance around the room to see who else is there.

B.) say I'm going to the restroom so I can talk to someone who looks interesting.

C.) give my date my undivided attention.

D.) secretly give my number to a hot prospect when my date is in the restroom.

_____ 2. I think about my ex

    A.) very rarely or never; I have better things to think about.

    B.) a lot, but that will change as soon as I meet someone new.

    C.) only when I think about sex.

    D.) only when I feel lonely or something reminds me of him or her.

_____ 3. My expectations for a relationship are as follows:

    A.) I'll live my life just the same as I do now, only happier.

    B.) I'll take care of me, and my partner will take care of himself or herself.

    C.) When I meet the right person, everything will fall into place.

    D.) I don't have any expectations; I just want someone to have fun with.

_____ 4. What I bring to a relationship is

    A.) my time and affection.

    B.) some issues, but nothing that can't be lived with.

    C.) flexibility—I can be whatever my partner wants me to be.

    D.) the knowledge that though I am not perfect, I am a great catch.

_____ 5. What I'm primarily looking for in a mate is

    A.) someone to take care of me.

    B.) someone who matches my specific wants and needs.

    C.) someone who will love me.

    D.) someone to have fun and great sex with.

_____ 6. My idea of a perfect night

    A.) is good company and great conversation.

    B.) is going out for drinks and hooking up.

    C.) means doing anything at all with the person I love.

D.) involves all my friends together in the same place.

___ 7. I think sex is

    A.) great, and the more the merrier!

    B.) best within a committed relationship.

    C.) something I don't think about all that often.

    D.) fun between consenting adults, and it doesn't have to be exclusive.

___ 8. When I think about living "happily ever after," I feel

    A.) that I will, with or without a partner.

    B.) that I never will; things never seem to work out for me.

    C.) optimistic that I will find the right partner to share my life with.

    D.) a little uneasy, as I'm not sure what that would be like.

___ 9. When I think of "till death do us part,"

    A.) I think it would depend on the partner.

    B.) I think that's an unrealistic expectation.

    C.) I think it means I'd never have to date again.

    D.) I'm hopeful I'll make that commitment to someone.

___ 10. The primary reason I want to meet someone new is that

    A.) I'm lonely and tired of being alone.

    B.) I'm ready to make a commitment and share my life with someone special.

    C.) I'm horny and I want to have sex.

    D.) It would be nice to have someone special to go places with.

Now go back and place a score on the line in front of the number for each of your choices:

For questions 1 and 6:

A = 3 points

B = 1 point

C = 5 points

D = 0 points

For questions 2 and 8:

A = 5 points

B = 0 points

C = 3 points

D = 1 point

For questions 3 and 7:

A = 1 points

B = 5 point

C = 0 points

D = 3 points

For questions 4 and 9:

A = 3 points

B = 1 point

C = 0 points

D = 5 points

For questions 5 and 10:

A = 0 points

B = 5 point

C = 1 points

D = 3 points

Enter your total score here:

My Total Score _____

What Your Score Means

If you scored 0–16, you're not ready for dessert. You're not ready to date. You have some issues that will keep you from having a happy partnership with anyone. No one can love you until you truly love yourself. Like attracts like, so while you're less than whole, you're attracting people who are less than whole. That combination creates a lot of dysfunction.

The best thing for you to do is take a break from dating and concentrate on yourself. Pamper yourself. Do all the things you have been neglecting. Do all of the quizzes and exercises in this book, and do some soul searching about the things you discover. Write your thoughts in your journal.

If you scored 17–25, you can have a little dessert if you eat it in moderation. You should only date occasionally. You have a few issues to work out before you can create a healthy relationship. If you're honest that you're not looking for anything serious, dating might be good practice for you. Just make sure you keep your focus on yourself. Limit dating to only once or twice a week. Keep it light and fun, and don't make any commitments or make it all about sex.

If you scored 26–39, dessert would probably be better for you than a full meal. You're just looking for some fun. You're not ready to make a commitment to someone. Casual dating is a great way to have fun while practicing your dating skills. It's easier to maintain your power and stand up for yourself when you're just in like, not in love. Take the opportunity to learn new things from several different people. Explore who you are and what you really want.

If you scored 40–50, you're ready for a well-balanced meal. You are ready for a serious relationship. You are taking responsibility for your thoughts and actions, you know what you want, and you love yourself. As long as you're willing to compromise and keep the relationship your priority, you'll probably be a good partner. Congratulations, you're a well-balanced meal!

Resources List

Organizations

Al-Anon Family Groups: http://www.al-anon.org.

Alcoholics Anonymous: http://aa.org.

Love Addicts Anonymous:
http://www.loveaddicts.org/LAAHomeIndex.html

National Domestic Violence Hotline: 1-800-799-SAFE.

http://www.thehotline.org.

Sex and Love Addicts Anonymous: http://slaafws.org.

Print Resources

Allen, Dr. Patricia, and Sandra Harmon. *Getting to "I Do": The Secret to Doing Relationships Right!*. New York: Quill, 2002.

Beattie, Melody. *Codependent no more: How to stop controlling others and start caring for yourself*. Center City, MN: Hazelden, 1987.

Carter, Steven, and Julia Sokol. *He's Scared, She's Scared: Understanding the Hidden Fears that Sabotage Your Relationships*. New York: Delacorte Press, 1995.

Carter, Steven, and Julia Sokol. *Men Who Can't Love: How to Recognize a Commitmentphobic Man Before He Breaks Your Heart*. New York: Berkley, 2000.

Chopich, Erika J., and Margaret Paul. *Healing Your Aloneness: Finding Love and Wholeness through Your Inner Child*. San Francisco: Harper & Row, 1990.

Edelman, Sarah. *Change Your Thinking: Overcome Stress, Combat Anxiety, & Depression, and Improve Your Life with CBT**. Cambridge, MA: Marlowe & Company, 2007.

Gawain, Shakti. *Creative Visualization: Use the Power of Your Imagination to Create What You Want in Your Life*. 25th anniversary ed. Berkeley, CA: New World Library, 2002.

Goleman, Daniel. *Emotional Intelligence: Why It Can Matter More Than IQ.* 10th anniversary ed. New York: Bantam Books, 2005.

Goleman, Daniel. *Social Intelligence: The New Science of Human Relationships.* New York: Bantam Books, 2006.

Hendrix, Harville. *Getting the Love You Want: A Guide for Couples.* 20th anniversary ed. New York: H. Holt, 2008.

Mellody, Pia; Andrea Wells Miller; and Keith Miller. *Facing Love Addiction: Giving Yourself the Power to Change the Way You Love: The Love Connection to Codependence.* New York, NY: HarperCollins, 1992.

Nhat Hanh, Thich. *Anger: Wisdom for Cooling the Flames.* New York: Riverhead Books, 2001.

Ratey, John J., and Albert M. Galaburda. *A User's Guide to the Brain: Perception, Attention, and the Four Theaters of the Brain.* New York: Pantheon Books, 2001.

Whitfield, Charles L. *Boundaries and Relationships: Knowing, Protecting, and Enjoying the Self.* Deerfield Beach, FL: Health Communications, Inc., 1993.

Woititz, Janet Geringer. *The Intimacy Struggle.* Deerfield Beach, FL: Health Communications, 1993.

Web Resources

Begley, Sharon. "The Brain: How the Brain Rewires Itself." Time. Dec. 3, 2012. http://www.time.com/time/magazine/article/0,9171,1580438,00.html.

Love and sex with Dr. Laura Berman: www.drlauraberman.com.

ABOUT THE AUTHOR

Donna Barnes, received life and relationship coach certification at New York University. She has written advice columns for *New York Moves* magazine, the *South Beach News*, RunningWithHeels.com, and LoveEngineer.com.

Donna was the on-air life and relationship coach for ABC News' top-rated magazine series *What Would You Do?* for three seasons. She has been a contributor on *Good Morning America*, CNN, NBC's *Today*, CBS's *Early Show*, Fox News, and Fuse; and she taught the girls how to "rock at love" on VH-1's *Rock of Love Charm School*. Donna has also provided more than four hundred relationship advice videos for eHow.com.

Cablevision's Metro TV in New York City dubbed Donna the "Dating Expert" when they chose her to cohost *Naked New York with Bob Berkowitz* in 2002–2003. Donna interviewed some of the country's top sex and relationship experts during its 205 episodes; it became Metro TV's top-rated show.